June Bill —

Love —

David

Fall '91

LIGHT ON THE SUBJECT
*Stage Lighting for Directors and Actors
—and the Rest of Us*

LIGHT ON THE SUBJECT

Stage Lighting
for Directors and Actors
—and the Rest of Us

DAVID HAYS

With an introduction by
PETER BROOK

LIMELIGHT EDITIONS
NEW YORK

Second Limelight Edition   March 1991
Copyright © 1989 by David Hays

Published by arrangement with Seagull Books, Calcutta

All rights reserved under international and Pan-American
Copyright Conventions.
Published in the United States by
Proscenium Publishers Inc., New York, and
simultaneously in Canada by
Fitzhenry & Whiteside, Limited, Toronto

Cover design by Jack Eckstein with Vermeer's
"Young Woman with a Water Jug" © 1983
by The Metropolitan Museum of Art, New York:
Gift of Henry G. Marquand, 1889,
Marquand Collection

Library of Congress Cataloging-in-Publication Data

Hays, David, 1930–
Light on the subject : stage lighting for directors and actors—
and the rest of us / David Hays.—1st Limelight ed.
p. cm.
Originally published: Calcutta : Seagull Books, 1988.
ISBN 0-87910-126-1 : $8.95
1. Stage lighting.   I. Title.
PN2091.E4H39 1989   89-12491
792'.025—dc20   CIP

Contents

Acknowledgements

My gratitude to Leonora, as always, and to Barbara Claire, Peter Hay, Jane Emerson, Naveen Kishore, Michael Sander, and Arthur Seelin; to collaborators through the years: Tharon Musser, John Gleason, Robert Benson, Charles Bugbee, Marvin March, Lowell Sherman, Fred Voelpel, Patricia Zipprodt, Peter Feller, Edward Bigelow, Rilla Bergman, Stephen Howe, Betty Beekman, Marshall Spiller, and Ronald Bates.

Introduction

We were sitting in the stalls of the Moscow Art Theatre, lighting *Hamlet*. This was many years ago, it was the very first visit of an English company to Moscow and the great Joe Davis, pioneer of theatre lighting in England, was giving his cues. As our lighting was very complex, the work went slowly and several hours had gone by while we carefully set up each cue. When the cue was right, we asked the Russian switchboard operators to note it down, unit by unit, on their plot. We had just reached cue 100 and it was 2 A.M.

"I think," Joe said prudently, "we should ask them to run the first hundred cues . . . just to see . . ."

"We're going back to cue 1," we called. "Cue 1, please!"

A long pause. Much discussion from the switchboard. A worrying hum of confusion in the air, lights switching on and off. Into our dismayed silence, a Russian voice:

"What does 'cue' mean?"

"Just give us again what you have written down," said Joe.

"We've written nothing down."

"Then what's on your plot?"

"What is a plot?"

Fortunately, Joe is a very calm man. Instead of cursing the hopeless inefficiency of all foreigners, he summoned the electricians from the board and gradually the complexity of the misunderstanding emerged. In the Moscow Art Theatre, a lighting plot was unknown. The electricians would be present at every rehearsal, which unlike our miserable four weeks would often last two years. They ended up knowing the play as well as the actors, and slowly built up the lighting stroke by stroke, day by day. When the performers came, they did not work by cues, they lived the lighting changes as the actor lived his entrances, his exits and his changing moods. Our reproaches died on our lips. We stood in awe in front of a superior way of work. However, the practical problem remained. We had only a few hours left. What could save the day?

"Can I help?" This time it was a very British intonation. I turned. Yes, someone had been sitting quietly in the dark all evening. I had taken him for a man from the Ministry of Culture. But as he rose to his feet and came forward and I saw gaiters, a flash of purple, I knew it was another form of ministry.

"May I introduce myself. I am the Bishop of Lambeth and Moscow. Yes, strange as it may seem, since the nineteenth century Moscow happens to be part of our diocese . . . I'm most interested in lighting, which is why I took the liberty of stopping by to watch . . ."

He began to remove his coat.

"When I was a young priest in Singapore, we did a lot of amateur theatricals. I always worked the switchboard and I would be happy to take over . . ."

We were torn between expediency and diplomacy. Politics won and we hung in with the Russians. By dawn we began to make headway. On the first night all went well, but the bishop in his shirt sleeves still stood by, ready at a glance to take over.

I recommend David's book as a contribution to the understanding of budding bishops, Russians and all fellow travellers in the search for light. Good luck to them.

PETER BROOK

I *This Book*

Stage lighting is not a black art. It can be practised openly. This book is dedicated to the directors, playwrights, actors, producers, critics, and set and costume designers who have feared its mysteries, and who have been pushed aside or discouraged in the formative years of school and stock. The insecurity of technicians and teachers can raise a wall of protective technical jargon and electrical folderol, and stifle gifted theatre people who might understand this work, contribute to it, and enjoy it more.

Come to the theatre. Did you see the last moments of Terence Rattigan's *Separate Tables?* The residents of a *pension* sit in frigid isolation under the harsh lights of their dining room. Events bring them to feel some sympathy for each other, and the angel of compassion enters the room. The harsh light dims. The tiny table lamps, unnoticed in the brightness, now cast their warm pools. The room, the characters, and the play are charmed as the curtain falls.

A good idea. Whose idea? The author's? The director's? Even—God forbid—an actors? Why not? Must ideas like this be the sole property of someone who knows how to calculate voltage drop in a series circuit?

This book is written so that even I can understand it. It is for those of you willing to grasp the notion that two fifty-watt bulbs add up to one hundred watts. Armed with no more than this ability to understand electricity, you can pass through the gate and join the club, the cheerful unintimidated, the slightly-more-perceptive, the helpful-without-meddling. This book won't make you into the artist who lights, for there is a threshold of instinct and artistry over which no bridegroom of a book can carry you. But you should understand what goes on in those particular brains, and what those special eyes seek. That's what this book hopes to tell you.

Sometimes I speak to you as if you are the director, sometimes

"A mild lemon light rinsed the streets."

—Saul Bellow

as if you are the designer, if that makes the conversation more simple.

This book is dedicated to theatre people like my wife Leonora, whose clear and bright mind snaps shut like a clam at the distant thunder of technical explanations.

There are few illustrations in this book. One is on page 17, where words truly failed, and I've drawn a little sketch. The other instruments and control devices are available to you, and better noted when you see them. Diagrams and cross-sections have a threatening quality that we don't need here.

There are anecdotes in this book. Small adventures, conversations. Mostly they're my adventures: I've had enough myself for our purpose. But this is not a memoir. There is a point to each story. We're talking here about attitudes, about what helps us create good work, about the feelings, often under tension, of this breed of artist.

To bring us closer together, most of the left-hand pages bear written descriptions of light in its appearance and its effects on us. The images may be useful to open and sharpen our thought. They add insight to sight. They are chosen from prose I've enjoyed. Poetry or drama can be as helpful, but are refined to one level beyond the articulation that most of us command.

During the production of *A Long Day's Journey into Night*, José Quintero asked for the kind of light that he saw or felt in shrouded Victorian rooms. In the buzzing stillness of summer afternoons the light seemed to him to hover, not touching walls, floor, or ceiling. Can we light a stage this way? No, but the image is provocative and nourishing.

Another image, from another director: "I want a warm wheat-colored feeling—wheat-colored." This phrase was no help. It had no bite, it suggested motion and a certain open light, but not in a useful image. It was vague and only fussed me.

Added to the explanations of procedure and instruments, and the quoted images, there is a glossary. This is for reference, not for intense study. It is surprisingly extensive for a technically simplified book, but is written in simple words. Plain language in the front of this book suggests plain language in the back. A serviceable glossary will be a companion to those of you who do not advance to other texts.

I've made a choice in the sequence within this book. Some prefer theory first, some prefer to start with the tools and hardware. I've chosen the second way—it combats awe.

The content of the chapters and the glossary will seem less elevated in tone than the fine thinking in the quotations. Yes, technical devices can seem silly when compared to high aims. Isn't that a point to be made in this book? Isn't that the nature of theatre? In Robert Edmond Jones' words:

Does this mean that we are to carry images of poetry and vision and high passion in our minds while we are shouting out orders to electricians on ladders in light rehearsals? Yes, this is what it means.[1]

---

[1]R. E. Jones, *The Dramatic Imagination.* New York: Theatre Arts Books, 1941, 1969, ch. vi.

2 Instruments I: Acting Light

Lighting instruments can be crudely divided into those used to light performers and those used to tone the stage or contribute to scenic effects. It's not a sharp distinction because many instruments in one category will do just fine in the other. But it helps to organize chapters like these, and it's handy in catalogues of equipment for sale.

We can start with the FOLLOW SPOT, an old favorite. Its sharp circle has become a symbol of theatre. In our ordinary language we say "Mrs. Jones will take the spotlight (or limelight—see Glossary) to describe the mating habits of the etc". You've seen follow spots at the back of the auditorium or you've seen their moving beams sweeping from a slot in the ceiling. An operator is loosely attached to each unit, and he or she "follows" the performers. "Follow" is a poor word—the operator should damn well be right abreast.

Follow spots don't always shoot from the front of the house. In opera, many musicals, and occasionally in dance and plays, they can be placed inside the proscenium. This shortens the light's long journey from the ceiling of a large auditorium. Hitting from the side can also cast the familiar circle and shadow, or the bounce off the floor, towards the wings instead of straight back on the scenery. Without a powerful beam in her eye, the diva can more easily sneak glances at the prompter. From these side positions we can also work subtly, and you may be unaware that the soft glow on a performer's face is from a follow spot.

The old standard follow spots are arcs. The light source is a brilliant steady spark that jumps the gap between two electrified carbon rods. It has a lot more zing than the spark made when you shake hands after walking on a new rug, but the principle is not altogether different: electricity leaps from a glutted place to a receptive one. The gap to be jumped is critical, therefore the carbon rods must be fed towards each other frequently and meticulously as they are consumed. This is called trimming the arc. The operator can see his work through

"Then a tremendous flash of light cut across the sky. Mr Tanimoto has a distinct recollection that it travelled from east to west, from the city toward the hills. It seemed a sheet of sun."

—John Hersey

a tiny porthole of dark glass. Bad trimming makes the spark flutter and fall short in its leap, with a disconcerting loud noise like a huge toilet flushing.

Follow spots are big because they contain space for air circulation around the intensely hot bluish-white source. The snouts are often long to contain lenses spaced apart as in a telescope. Beam-shaping devices can be in this snout: an iris to open or close the circle of light, or shutters to change the circle into a rectangle which can widen to full stage. Holders with different color filters live in here, and can quickly swing into the path of light. There still is that critical moment at the end of the strip tease when the blue is needed, and fast.

Tending this open, flowing spark is a tricky business. There are new lamps (bulbs) as powerful as arcs: in fact they are arcs, contained in the gas-filled glass bulb, and they work without constant adjustment. The gas nourishes the rods and they don't wear down. Also, less powerful conventional incandescent lamps can be used for shorter throws. These don't need elaborate, and often noisy, cooling fans, and have the advantage of dimming. There are ways of dimming an arc, but not by easing the current: if you did this the spark wouldn't jump. You have to do it mechanically. You throw the beam into wide focus, and this means that the output of light is spread over a wide area and therefore diluted or weakened at any one point. At the same time, you can close the iris to keep the circle the same size on stage. Within this same size circle, the light is weaker. It's a neat trick, usually combining fun and failure. One operates the iris with a handle that sticks out, and it closes like the iris in a camera lens.

When you see tiny Tinkerbell spots of lights darting around the proscenium or curtain before the show begins, you know the operators are trimming their arcs and warming up. They've got to be ready to pick up Mr. Joy as he steps out of the wings. They should know when he's to appear, from exactly where, and his speed of travel. If they know he's only four foot eleven, they won't score a clean miss over his head. It requires rehearsal and skill to land that pinpoint on his face and spread it smoothly over all of him as he strides along.

This is a good place to talk about lamps. "Lamp" is our mys-

"Nearly midnight. The hour when an invalid, who has been obliged to start on a journey and to sleep in a strange hotel, awakens in a moment of illness and sees with glad relief a streak of daylight showing under his bedroom door. Oh, joy of joys! it is morning. The servants will be about in a minute: he can ring, and someone will come to look after him. The thought of being made comfortable gives him strength to endure his pain. He is certain he heard footsteps: they come nearer, and then die away. The ray of light beneath his door is extinguished. It is midnight; someone has turned out the gas; the last servant has gone to bed, and he must lie all night in agony with no one to bring him any help."

—Marcel Proust

tery word for "light bulb". You're already familiar with the three major parts. The "bulb" means only the glass part—the round (globular) or pear-shaped or tubular glass envelope. Inside this is the second major part, the filament. Both of these parts are attached to the third major part, the base. There are new breeds of stage lamps now, with names like quartz or tungsten-halogen, and some of these look like the barrels of hypodermic needles, and snap into holders at both ends.

Here are three lamp thoughts at this moment. First, the smaller the filament, the more accurately can a reflector redirect its light. Small intense sources are usually a good thing when the instrument has a reflector. Second, the filament should be aligned perfectly with the reflector for best results. That's why we rarely use household screw bases: they're sloppy and end up any old way. In theatre you'll usually find controlled snap-ins, or pins-into-holes, or twist and lock bases. Third, some lamps must burn in a certain position: base up, base down. This is because the glass bulb will melt unless it keeps its proper distance from the hot filament. Filaments can also cast off particles which slowly blacken the inside of the glass. There are now gases in some lamps which have a retarding or even a healing effect on this disease. Other improvements are arriving, and from time to time these are put into circulation by firms that hate spoiling us with lamps that last too long.

Let's return to our instruments. The ELLIPSOIDAL REFLECTOR SPOT and the FRESNEL are the real workhorses in the actor-lighting department. In the first, the ERS or ellipsoidal, there is an ellipsoidally-shaped reflector. The lamp pokes into this through a hole, and the wrap-around reflector, which looks like half a football, snares a large part of the light and sends it through lenses which condense it further to a narrow and strong beam. This beam is sharp-edged, but you can fuzz it (blur the focus) by moving the instrument's snout. With this instrument you can cut light off the proscenium and apron cleanly, with a minimum of stray light tickling the big hairdos in the first row. There are movable metal strips inside the barrel of the unit, called framing shutters or "cut-offs". These are controlled by handles which you push to slice off unwanted parts of the round beam. You can pare off the light over the actors' heads,

"The light inside the train was not particularly strong, and the reflection was not as clear as it would have been in a mirror. Since there was no glare, Shimamura came to forget that it was a mirror he was looking at. The girl's face seemed to be out in the flow of the evening mountains.

It was then that a light shone in the face. The reflection in the mirror was not strong enough to blot out the light outside, nor was the light strong enough to dim the reflection. The light moved across the face, though not to light it up. It was a distant, cold light. As it sent its small ray through the pupil of the girl's eye, as the eye and the light were superimposed one on the other, the eye became a weirdly beautiful bit of phosphorescence on the sea of evening mountains."

—Yasunari Kawabata

or move in one, two, three or all four sides to frame to a door or a platform or a portrait of the long-gone husband.

This precise control over a narrow bright beam suggests these instruments for use in the front-of-house (the auditorium), and that's where you see them, on the balcony rails or on the stands set up in the boxes or on the side walls, where boxes used to be. (We call these positions "Box Booms".) Often you see an added snout, called a top hat, and this stops bits of stray light that careen off dust or faults in the lens.

Because of the extra devices and careful manufacture, these instruments are a touch heavy, and costly. They're made in different sizes and powers, and are named by their lens diameter, their wattage, and their focal length. This last choice isn't complicated, and "narrow spread" or "wide spread" usually tells the electrician or supplier what you want.[1] The smallest ellipsoidals have a three-and-one-half-inch diameter lens, and the biggest for large stage use is a twelve-inch unit. Wattages range from four hundred to two thousand. Usually we use the six- or eight-inch size, with a seven-fifty or one-thousand watt lamp. Bigger sizes are generally for effects like sunbeams, or for huge theatres. From the auditorium (the front) you might want the narrow beam, but onstage, from above or from the wings, you may need the wider spread to cover more actors or all of one big one.

One common name for the Ellipsoidal Reflector Spot is Leko, but that's a trade name, an acronym made from two men's names. You don't find the ERS everywhere. A front-of-house unit that I've used happily in many countries in Europe, in Australia and in the Far East combines the qualities of the ERS and the Fresnel, the next unit we discuss. The beam is powerful, wide or narrow, sharp or soft-edged. You lack the cut-offs, but life seems to go on without them.

Our second great workhorse, the FRESNEL, is named after the French physicist Augustin Fresnel (1788–1827), who developed this lens style towards the improvement of lighthouses. The

[1]New ERS units are being made with a great range of focusing ability, like camera zoom lenses. You may not have to specify narrow or wide spread: one unit may do for all.

"In Chang during a fire (some wood prepared for the construction of a catholic mission was burning) I saw an elderly Chinese at a safe distance from the fire throwing water assiduously, determinedly and without tiring over the reflection of the flames on the walls of his dwelling . . ."

—Vladimir Nabokov

fresnel is simpler, lighter in weight, and cheaper than the ellipsoidal. It has a wide, soft-edged beam. Much has been made of this soft edge, or even the softness in the center of the beam. There is a difference seen by the keen-eyed in certain circumstances and a big fresnel can be nice for moonlight. But remember that an ellipsoidal can also be made soft-edged.

The lamp in a fresnel is mounted on a metal holder, or carriage. The reflector is attached to this same carriage. The light that hits this reflector is sent right back through the filament, and the filament and reflector always keep this fixed relationship. You push or crank the carriage forward towards the lens for a wide beam or back from the lens for a narrow beam. We say we flood the unit[1] for the wide beam and spot it for the narrow beam. Even though you can't cut off the edges of the beam sharply as in an ellipsoidal, you can easily make the entire field of light wider or narrower.

Fresnels start with a baby—we call them "inkies"—with a three-inch diameter lens and a lamp as gentle as seventy-five watts. This unit, like the tiny ellipsoidal, might fit into a small space, perhaps on a low ceiling, or tucked into a porch post onstage. I've used three-inch inkies as footlights to smooth out wrinkled faces. Big stage fresnels can be twelve inches and two-thousand watts, a fine unit for high-mounted toplight or side light. Five-thousand watt sixteen-inch units are common in television and film. The ones we ordinarily meet for small stages have a six-inch diameter lens with five-hundred or seven-hundred-and-fifty watt lamps. Eight- or ten-inch units at one-thousand watts are common for normal stages.

Because fresnels throw a relatively wide and soft beam, with lots of stray light, they aren't much use out in the house. They do their best work on the first pipe (I'll explain that), or for downlight, or for soft wide beams from the side for dance. They can be focused more easily and quickly than ellipsoidals because there are fewer devices to control, but this is a trap: they can take longer if you try to use them where an ellipsoidal is needed. If you must have sharp cut-offs, you may waste everyone's time cutting out tinfoil or being finicky with barn doors,

[1]Unit means instrument—a single instrument.

"The arches of the bridges leap into light; the moon clocks glow . . ."

—Dylan Thomas

which are metal flaps, like horse blinders, that cut off stray light.

A plus for fresnels is the ease with which their soft-edged beam blends with other light fields. An actor won't seem to step through a hard line as he walks from the light of one instrument into the light of another. This and the wide angle are important in low-ceilinged rooms, or if you have few instruments. However, the beam of an ellipsoidal can be softened and blended. Don't underrate it.

About lenses: they change the direction of light, and for theatre purposes we say they concentrate the light. This means that they catch the light from the filament or reflector and redirect it in a narrower beam towards the stage. If lenses didn't do this, the light could be stopped by frames or baffles so that it didn't spread all over, but that light would be wasted instead of channelled. There are plenty of lenses in nature, and you see this redirection of light every time you reach into the water for your golf ball. Your arm seems to shoot off in another direction.

Augustin Fresnel, no golfer, knew that light beams are bent at the entry point when they move from one medium to another. For example, light bends when it enters glass or water from air—and when it exits. Lenses had been around for centuries. But, reasoned Fresnel, if the action is on the surfaces, why bother with thick glass in between? Thick glass is heavy, hard to cast perfectly, and cracks under heat. Fresnel kept the curved surfaces of the lens in the same relationship, but reduced the glass between. See the sketch—here simple words do fail. See that the lens jogs back every so often: it starts the curve, steps back, continues the curve, steps back again, etc. (A variation of Fresnel's invention is, in fact, called a Step Lens. It's in the glossary, and not important except to lens buffs.)

As I write this I can see a lighthouse with a fresnel lens system, made by Henry LePaute in Paris soon after the turn of the century. The whole assembly— the lamp, the lenses, and their holders—rotates on a bed of mercury. The clockwork weights that turn the system descend forty feet in an iron tube that forms the structural spine of the lighthouse. The lenses are beautiful and I've climbed the tower many times to

"... at any rate, it is worth reporting that long before the circus comes to town, its most notable performances have already been given. Under the bright lights of the finished show, a performer need only reflect the electric candle power that is directed upon him, but in the dark and dirty old training rings and in the makeshift cages, whatever light is generated, whatever excitement, whatever beauty, must come from original sources—from internal fires of professional hunger and delight, from the exuberance and gravity of youth. It is the difference between planetary light and the combustion of stars."

—E. B. White

see them. Too big to be cast as a single piece, they are made in curved strips like wedge-shaped Venetian blinds, and held perfectly in place at just the right angles by polished brass supports. The lenses are so effective that the beam is rated conservatively at nineteen nautical miles, even though the light source surrounded by these lenses is only a two-hundred-and-fifty-watt lamp.

Another unit in our arsenal is a mounted REFLECTOR LAMP. These lamps have a mirror surface coated on the inside of the bulb, in perfect permanent relationship to the filament. Your auto headlights are reflector lamps, and you've seen ceiling lights and outdoor lights with names like R-40 or PAR 56.

These lamps, which can't change focus, have a variety of holders ranging from a metal strap device, which looks like a chastity belt, to a sturdy professional casing. These casings have barn doors which give you some control over the beam spread. You choose this angle of spread when you order reflector lamps, and some models have a useful oval field of light. Some have a color cast in the glass itself.

These units have a lot of punch and are simple. Where exact control isn't needed, they're a delight to use. We sometimes call them PARCANS; just a nickname for the way they look and the way we made them when we were broke—a socket stuck in a number-ten can.

There is one more unit that could fit into this chapter, though it is more often used for simple projected effects. This is the old PLANO-CONVEX SPOT. Looks like a boxy fresnel. The lens is a solid piece of curved glass, not stepped. They can be spotted or flooded like a fresnel, and their beams can be cut off rather precisely by tinfoil or barn doors. A pattern (leaves etc.) can be placed in front, on the lens. The old-fashioned appearance of the units is interesting on stage, and once we used them in *Woyzeck*, with actors pushing them around to light each scene. But if you never see an old P.C., your life won't be incomplete.

"They had turned off the lights, and in the big room illumined only from the terrace there rested pools of darkness between the windows. As they moved I lost their faces and found them again. At one moment the shadows gave my aunt a deceptive air of youth: she looked like the young woman in my father's photograph pregnant with happiness, and at another I recognized the old woman who had faced Miss Paterson with such merciless cruelty and jealousy . . . A flashbulb broke the shadows up. I have the photograph still—all three of us are petrified by the lightning flash into a family group."

—Graham Greene

3 Instruments II: Effects

Moving into the wash and tone department, the old standby is the STRIPLIGHT. You've seen them as footlights or hung overhead in school theatres. An ancient and rotten model is a row of sockets holding lamps dipped in amber, green, blue, or red syrup (there are better colored glass lamps now available). Better yet are sectioned troughs with a lamp in each section. There should be a color holder for each compartment. It's sad to see school theatres still equipped with only these units to glow on the dim children. True, all of this has a noble heritage: rows of candles once decked the aprons and hid behind the lip of every wing. But footlights, if you depend on them, produce an unearthly upward blaze on the actors, which then splits into fruity-colored shadows on the backdrop. Meanwhile the overhead striplights force the actors upstage and they stand, lit straight up and down in the pasty incandescent vise. But at least footlights are near an actor's face, if there's nothing better out front. Used carefully, footlights can enhance dancers' legs and wash out shadows under a chin or two. The slight tone that will reach up from foots to tint borders or wings can be helpful.

There wasn't much choice years ago when there were no spotlights to reach you from the front except our friend, the follow spot. The footlight was wonderfully theatrical; look at Degas' pastels of café singers with up-shooting light. Light from strips spilled upstage evenly, with no ability to sculpt a chair or a balustrade. The tradition of painting even the furniture on the backdrop worked well enough. Today the good striplights are powerful light sources. They use reflector lamps or quartz lamps in each compartment.

Strips can be used for toning skies. Slung to overhead pipes, they can also tone acting areas and they have the virtue of being skinny: when you're loaded in the flys they don't take up much room. Strips are quickly hung and easily tilted in the right general direction. That's their disadvantage for downstage use—their broad wash spills where you don't want it. Down-

"But all these three rooms are dark, for that matter. It is partly because of the set of the windows, but it is still more that the once whitewashed walls are so dirty. They have in the course of years absorbed smoke and grease and dirt into a rich dark patine so laboured into the wood that sweeping and scrubbing affect it as scarcely as if it were iron; so that even in the kitchen, where two windows are not shaded with porch or trees, but are free to the sky's whole blaze, the brightness though powerful is restricted, fragile and chemical like that of a flash bulb, and is blunted or drowned in the iron blackness of every wall."

—James Agee

stage, a row of fresnels or parcans may be needed for better control.

Striplights, or any instruments toning a backdrop, can light from behind, assuming that the fabric or plastic is translucent—or transparent with applications that catch light. Theatre netting such as "scrim" can take on wonderfully different qualities when hit from front, back—or both.

Striplights are usually named by their size and the number of lamps they hold. Thus a "six-by-twelve" is a strip about six inches wide, twelve lamps long. If each lamp is in its own compartment, and these compartments are square, the strip will be about six feet long. The lamps will be linked (circuited) together and in a three-circuit striplight this means that the first, fourth, seventh, and tenth lamps will be joined as one circuit; the second, fifth, eighth, and eleventh the second; and the rest the third. Three plugs will pop out of each end of the unit, and if you hang five or six of them along one pipe you can just plug them end to end like incandescent sausages and you have an instant stage-wide row of three separately controlled colors. (This is not the best way to cable: three individual cables to each unit is better and safer practice, though obviously more fussy, heavier, and requiring much more cable.)

Often two or three pipes of striplights are hung to light the sky when you need good intensity and must vary the color. If they're too far from the sky, they'll wash it evenly but weakly. If they're too close, the sky will be bright on top and weak half way down, and you may get a saw-tooth as the alternating colors hit the cloth before the beams have room to spread and merge.

We often use strips upstage as floor units to light a sky. They can be called horizon strips. Shooting up, the rising heat will quickly melt gel and plastic color filters, so colored glass is useful. These strips can be concealed behind a scenic ground row or can hide in a trench cut for that purpose in the stage.

There's a little instrument similar to a striplight that we call a BACKING STRIP. It's small, narrow and light, with only a few compartments, usually circuited together. It fits neatly over a door and can light a hallway or backing. The good ones have color holders. It's dandy.

Less dandy and still seen hanging over older stages or concert

"We put our possessions in a wagon and rode to Radzymin, and even though I was only three at the time, I remember the journey . . . we rode through fields, forests, and past windmills. It was a summer evening, and the sky seemed ablaze with blowing coals, fiery brooms, and beasts. There was a buzzing, a humming, and the croaking of frogs. The wagon had halted, and I saw a train, first a large locomotive with three lamps like suns, then freight cars trailing behind in a slow, preoccupied way. They seemed to come from nowhere and to go beyond the end of the world, where the darkness loomed."

—Isaac Bashevis Singer

stages is a huge trough with white lamps in a row. This can light a full-stage gathering for *The Messiah,* help you strike the platforms afterwards and is called a CONCERT BORDER and is also called a damn nuisance when you're trying to cram in drops and spotlights for a drama or musical. But it's better than one solo lamp as a worklight for rehearsals.

SCOOPS or FLOODLIGHTS are useful for flopping light on drops or backings. These are lensless, and usually come in diameters of ten to eighteen inches; just big reflectors that look like aluminium mixing bowls with color holders. The older ones have a big lamp in the middle, and some new units use a powerful quartz lamp, are more carefully made, and even have a device to adjust the spread of their beam. You've seen small powerful versions at the photographer's and we're using those more and more on stage.

Sometimes scoops are hung between sections of striplights or at the ends of these pipes, where they reinforce the color washes or reach down to the center of the sky where the strips fade. This kind of fill-in work can often be done from the wings, and a small traveling show that can't depend on overhead lights might use scoops on stands, instead of strips, to light the backgrounds. Scoops might also add the exotic colors so that we can use most of the striplights for blues.

A small scoop might perch over a doorway or window like a backing strip, and light a hallway or a small window backing.

Incidentally, in the antique department, there is a boxy thing called an OLIVETTE, with one huge lamp, which pours light onstage from a stand in the wings. The old BUNCHLIGHT does the same, but worse. It has many lamps screwed into sockets on a white pan and is mentioned here because the name is funny. But in film work, units such as the "Nine-Light" (nine powerful reflector lamps on a rectangular holder) are just fine. Each lamp has a switch: you have nine grades of intensity. We sometimes envy the film lighting designer, who can walk up to the units any time, off camera.

After STRIPS and SCOOPS, the basic wash and tone units, we can proceed to more specific effect units. First, the BEAM PROJECTOR, which throws a narrow intense shaft of light, so narrow that it hardly widens at all. It can be used to stimulate sunbeams

"What a profound silence! Not a single bird-note was heard in the sky over this grave in the hollow of the mountains. Only a lonely light lingered on the cedars and mountain. By and by the light gradually grew fainter, till the cedars and bamboo were lost to view. Lying there, I was enveloped in deep silence.

Then someone crept up to me. I tried to see who it was. But darkness had already been gathering round me. Someone . . . that someone drew the small sword softly out of my breast in its invisible hand. At the same time once more blood flowed into my mouth. And once and for all I sank down into the darkness of space."

—Ryunosuke Akutagawa

or searchlights. It is, in fact, a small version of the classic sky-probing searchlights. The common stage sizes are ten or sixteen inches in diameter, and look like shallow coffee cans with dished-out backs. These curved backs are the reflectors, parabolic in shape. There is no lens: the light from the lamp springs forward from the reflector. Concentric rings and shields in the unit block any wandering light.

Beam projectors can be used elaborately in stacks, perhaps with the color starting thin on top and deepening as one goes down so that by careful cross-fading you can change the angle and the color for a sunset. What a luxury! They can create forest or cathedral light shafts too.

An interesting but limited unit, and it's sad to see so many sold to schools and rarely dusted off. It has a distinctive quality if well used, and so it survives.

EFFECT PROJECTORS are worth several books in themselves. They project images ranging from water ripples to leaves to lettering to exact landscapes or architecture in full photographic illusion. They can project on—and alter—an actor's body. From time to time one hears the unpleasant rumor that they will replace all scenery (except, one assumes, the frightfully expensive screens needed for reflection of their images). At any but the top level of professional work, trust your common sense. When you see the slides of Aunt Ethel's vacation, note that she dims the lights in the room. So must it be on stage. If your actors keep away from the projection surface (the screen or backdrop), and if you take infinite pains to keep bounce light from straying on to it, you could still be disappointed. It looks seductively effective from production photographs, but perhaps the acting light was dimmed for the photographer. I'd ask for that, wouldn't you? Is it worth giving up the blood-quickening hot light of Verona that strikes directly on Tybalt and Mercutio in order to see a background postcard of Verona that's too pale anyway? It is possible to do this well, but it's time-consuming and costly.

It's also hard to keep the unity of a production intact when you use projections. Recently we saw some expert work at the Metropolitan Opera in New York. The opera was by Wagner and murky, so the projected landscape, complete with a moving

"He replaced the stump in the candlestick with a new candle, put it on the window sill, and lit it. The flame choked and sputtered, shooting off small stars, and sharpened to an arrow. A soft light filled the room. In the sheet of ice covering the windowpane a black eyelet began to form at the level of the flame."

—Boris Pasternak

waterfall, was real enough to walk in, or nearly so. I was fascinated, every moment. But realism aside, the forest scene was dull as dishwater—hard as it is to make a clearing dreary—and I remembered the legendary story, "Sir, you have a chance to direct a play on double treadmills!" "Young man, what are they *saying* on the treadmills?" Later in the opera, we came to the Great Hall scene, and there was no way to project it. The set no longer seemed merely real enough to touch it; it was real and it was touched, and the unity of the scenic conception collapsed.

I like projections, and have used them for scene-opening pictures like visual epigraphs, and in situations where the actors were hit by the projected light, and passed through dappled leaves or shafts tinted by stained glass. In theatre-in-the-round this is particularly useful, because you lack conventional scenery, and the effect is on, not behind, the actors. But when acting light comes on, the projector's intensity must be enormous, and if you haven't got the punch, you must sneak in these effects during transitions when the actors' light is low, and the backs are turned. Besides the need for great intensity, there is rarely room for long throws. So wide-angle lenses must be used. These lenses must be skillfully made and mounted, the slides meticulously adapted to counteract the fishbowl distortion.

There is a crude projector called a LINNEBACH, a lamp inside a black box, shining out through a big sheet of glass or plastic that forms one side of the box. You can paint this sheet in bold simple silhouette patterns. This seemed just right to create a storm on a big plaster cyc that I enjoyed using with Sarah Caldwell when we were in the opera department at Tanglewood. At the right moment we had our storm over the desert, looking like a great frozen marble cake. The tenor rushed out into the storm like Lear and waited for his re-entrance, crouched behind the big box. He picked his nose, and we saw this thirty feet high, with a clarity of detail that filled me with pride, depressed Sarah, and seemed to delight the audience.

Another simple projector is our friend from the last chapter, the ellipsoidal reflector spot. You can fit a cut-out metal pattern in place of the framing shutters. Small area patterns such as leaf patches or Venetian blinds can be sharp and bright.

In film or television work, big cut-outs to mottle the light can be held in front of the powerful units, and these are called GOBOES or CUKES.

Sometimes a perforated wheel in front of a lens can be spun to give a ripple or flicker, and we call these simple devices LOBSTERSCOPES. In more sophisticated projectors, a wheel or film loop inside the lens system can show us water ripples, racing storm clouds and so forth. Here we come to the fabulous and costly instruments, including a full range of film projection from multiple positions. Slide projectors similar to those used for your thirty-five millimeter camera transparencies are just fine, but may need special lenses, intense sources, and beefed-up (and then quietened down) cooling systems. You see these in the thrilling work of Alwin Nikolais's dance company. But remember that Nick is designing and composing and choreographing at the same time. His projections work as projections, and not as a substitute for another reality. He often projects on the dancers themselves, creating costume variations. His effects always relate directly and closely to the business at hand—his dancers.

In the picture books about décor we see wonders of quality projections. Some effects you simply can't get in other ways, such as swiftly changing newspaper headlines or rapid shifts of locale or abstract patterned color that make you feel as if you are at the movies. But this work is in its infancy. Stages are starting to pop and bubble and burst with light—in the scenery, hitting it, and on actors and audiences. Holograms may bring extraordinary spectacle to us. And I believe that great actors will still be with us in these marvels-to-be.

4 The Hook-up

We've now noted the basic instruments—let's plug them in. This is simple, easily compared to plugging in a lamp or toaster at home. The trouble is the ornate labeling, an appetizer in our feast of confusion. It's not the nomenclature of nuclear physics, but it sounds like that when shouted across a dark auditorium. The user knows it and you don't, which is bad enough. Worse, it's often spoken in abbreviated terms. But it's a simple code, available to you if you want. There's little need for a director or actor to know all this, but please relax and realize that you're not hearing discussion at a doctoral level.

Hooking up or plugging in means connecting the lighting instruments to the dimmer board. The board supplies the electricity and varies its strength so that the lights will dim.

The simplest way to hook up is to connect each light directly to the board with its own cable. (Cable just means heavy duty extension cord.) But strings of cable, like great masses of spaghetti, have bulk and weight, and can be unsightly to the audience, a snare to movement around the stage, and illegal.

Therefore we can do what you do in your home, where you don't want every lamp to have a long cord leading down all the steps to the cellar source. You plug into wall receptacles. Your receptacles are wired to cables, which glide unseen through the walls to your home's power source.

A modern theatre, like a home, is full of waiting receptacles, handy to the lamps you want to connect. The receptacles have names, usually describing their location. Some typical names are Ceiling Cove, Balcony Front, Box Right, First Floor Pocket Left, or First Electric (this is a pipe hung above the stage). In each location, including the pipes, there will probably be several receptacles, and these are numbered. If there is the above-mentioned Ceiling Cove, which is a slot across the ceiling of the auditorium, there might be a receptacle placed every two or three feet—perhaps twenty receptacles. Therefore the label, "Ceiling Cove #16" is clear enough. If you know from which

"A clear starlight night throws such heavy shadows that, if you don't know the shape of a shore perfectly, you would claw away from every bunch of timber, because you would take the black shadow of it for a solid cape, and you see you would be getting scared to death every fifteen minutes by the watch. You would be fifty yards from shore all the time when you ought to be within fifty feet of it. You can't see a snag in one of those shadows but you know exactly where it is, and the shape of the river tells you when you are coming to it. Then there's your pitch-dark night; the river is a very different shape on a pitch-dark night from what it is on a starlight night. All shores seem to be straight lines then, and mighty dim ones too, and you'd *run* them for straight lines, only you know better. You boldly drive your boat right into what seems to be a solid, straight wall (you knowing very well that in reality there is a curve there) and that wall falls back and makes way for you. Then there's your grey mist. You take a night when there's one of these grisly, drizzly, grey mists, and then there isn't *any* particular shape to a shore. A grey mist would tangle the head of the oldest man that ever lived. Well, then, different kinds of *moonlight* change the shape of the river . . ."

—Mark Twain

end the number starts, and how many receptacles there are, you can guess approximately where the receptacle is.

What's the simple formula for finding out what these names mean? Ask, as I've asked, in South Bend, Singapore, and Sydney. The plugging nomenclature of any theatre breaks down simply, and usually with logic. If "Ceiling Cove #16" is shouted as "Cee-Cee-One-Six," you can still understand it if you really want to, or have to.

If an instrument's own short cable and plug can't reach, you use another short length of cable, often called a jumper, to plug it into the receptacle. If you plug into a receptacle on stage, called a stage pocket, there may be a metal flap on the floor covering the sunken receptacle, and there will probably be notches cut out of the edge of this flap so that you don't pinch the cable when you close it. Plugs often have twist-lock devices so that they can't pull out as easily as they do at home. When you've plugged into a receptacle, you've connected to a cable that slithers to some place near the dimmer board where it emerges, hopefully clearly labeled. You can now plug the instrument into the dimmer you've chosen.

Hold it—there may be another step involved, and don't let your mind snap shut. Imagine a hundred cables popping out of the floor near the dimmer board. A massive tangle, however clear the labelling. If the dimmer board is in a small booth at the back of the auditorium, it would be frightful to run all the cable back there. Thrashing about waist-deep in it would be worse, in that tiny room.

Therefore the cables don't just pop out of the floor. In a theatre with receptacles, they end in a device called a patch panel. This is like an old telephone switchboard. The cable becomes a plug, like a phone plug, and you can pull it up or down like Mollie at Central in the old movies, and then you can plug it into a hole (the "jack", oddly enough) which is connected to the dimmer of your choice. Each dimmer is represented by several holes so that you can plug different cables, each from a different receptacle if you wish, into one dimmer. This action at the patch panel is called patching. The panel can be placed anywhere where it's easy for the cable and stagehands to reach.

Let's go back on stage. What happens if we want to plug five lamps into a receptacle with four openings. There are various ways, and the simplest is to connect two instruments and then plug them as one into one receptacle. It's just like using the double socket at the end of your home extension cord. Our device doesn't look like that, but it works the same way. We call it a "Twofer" (two for one). We even have "threefers" but that gets nasty, and shouldn't happen.

When we're plugged, we tidy up. Cables or jumpers don't have to snag the scenery or trip the cast. We string them over our heads or cover them with rug runners.

Plugging is fun if you don't lose the labels. When it's complete, you might well run through the whole set-up to see that everything is where it should be, connected to the right dimmers. Then the focus can begin. This moment always frightens me. Butterflies suddenly hatch from a thousand cocoons in my system.

One designer I know always throws up at this moment. His solution is to start focusing just before lunch so that the least nourishment is lost. But it's like a plunge into cold water—it feels good when you finally do it. Just clutch that first instrument and aim it.

5 *The Focus*

You focus a lamp the way you shear a sheep—grab it with confidence. As in tennis or golf, your feet have to be planted just right. Place that ladder shrewdly. You shouldn't have to lean out too far, or duck to move your opaque head out of the path of light. People who care for you should steady the ladder.

There's no sense performing a delicate focus on a unit that intends to swivel down and hang limply the minute you let it go. So: is the pipe or stand secure? Will it rotate? Now tighten the basic clamp of the unit, which clamps the yoke to the pipe or stand. Next, hand-tighten the other handles. Now put the hot spot (center of the beam) where you want it. Someone is the target, and his or her eye might be more sensitive in finding the hot spot than the eye of the focuser. But no target should go blind by staring into the source. I like to turn away from the lamp and watch my head's shadow in the circle of light on the wall or floor.

Focus the center of the beam where you want the heat—the hottest spot. Then firmly tighten the other nuts or handles that hold the lamp just there. Then flood, spot, or work the cut-offs. This is the key—start by putting the hot spot where you want it. It's amateurish to place the edges of the circle of light neatly on stage and then hope the actors catch the bright part.

You might want gloves, particularly if the board operator isn't nimble enough to turn on only the lamps you need just as you need them. Perhaps many lamps (units) are plugged into one dimmer, or circuit. If you plug or unplug these lamps as you go, follow ordinary common sense. Turn off the juice, plug, then turn it on again. Pay attention at the board, and for everyone's sake find a way to stop that awful yelling. There are alternatives, such as simple hand signals, or walkie-talkie relaying. If communication is good with the board, and the board operator is alert, the focus goes twice as fast—this communication is the weak link.

The order of focusing is critical. Front-of-house units can be started before the set is up. Clever ways to reach pipes over tricky and ladder-resisting platforms should be prepared in advance. Above all, learn to focus with some light on stage. Don't force the set or prop crews to stop work. You'll see enough, and save more time for touch-up later. Leave the most easily reached units, such as low side booms, until the last.

Start an energizing rhythm and keep it moving. Don't get too fussy right away—some details that seriously interrupt the flow of work might be left until later. Remember what a fine painter and teacher, Horace Armistead, said about scene painting: First, draw carefully. Then mix your colors carefully. Select your brushes carefully. Then paint the cloth freely and swiftly: it's just the lay-in. When it dries, you can do the details freely and swiftly, because the lay-in was so good.

Hand focusing of units will be with us for a long time in ordinary situations, but remote control of focus and color is here, to be used for effects such as sweeping sheets of color-changing light, for speed and convenience for the key lights in a television studio, for following spots in difficult-to-man positions, etc. The technology will become cheaper, use will be encouraged for speed and safety and as a way (contested) to pinch off salaries, and some day this type of unit will be standard for many positions in a theater.

6 *The Light Plot*

The light plot shows you what to do. It's fun to draw because you use a little plastic stencil that neatly outlines each instrument. A complete light plot might be on one sheet chock full of information or on several sheets for bigger shows. Naturally, the light plot comes first, and specifies what instruments to use, where to put them, how to focus them, and how to plug them.

The first and most familiar sheet is the plan. You look down on the stage with all the instruments and the pipes and stands drawn in place and clearly named or numbered. Notes such as an instrument's wattage or color or purpose might be written down next to it or within its drawn outline. Different kinds of shading or cross-hatching can be used, and these symbols should be clearly explained on the sheet. Heights of the pipes or stands can be noted. The scale of the drawing should be set down. Actually, these plans are often not drawn to exact scale: some distances are compressed so that much can fit on one sheet of paper.

A second sheet might be a section, a side view of the stage. The section will probably be drawn to exact scale because it helps determine the true lengths of throws and the angles. The set designer would like to know what beams hit the actors and miss the scenery.

A third sheet or two is the instrument schedule, and this is hardcore hardware, and a turn-off for the casual observer. There are no pictures, just a lot of writing in columns about the instruments and everything you want to know about them, usually more than you could fit on the light plot. There's the exact size and style of the instrument, where it's hung, the exact lens, the wattage, the color, the type of clamp, special hardware such as a top hat, its combination with other instruments, what dimmer it's headed for, a note on its purpose (Act II sofa special, for example), and notes on its focus such as "shutter off chandelier", or "fit to door frame but soft-edge", or "rubber pad" if it's head height.

"Suddenly a change passed over the tree. All the sun's warmth left the air. I knew the sky was black, because all the heat which meant light to me, had died out of the atmosphere."

—Helen Keller

All of these drawings and lists set down clear information. Any abbreviations or trade name mysteries can be explained.

Sometimes the sheets are not clear and look like a yardful of chicken tracks. This can be either ordinary bad work, or elegant bad work in the stylish architectural forms which thumb their noses at the laymen. The A's are crossed so low that they look like triangles, the lines intersect and wander on instead of merely ending. This tradition of murk is useful if your friendly utility needs approval of its plans in a town meeting and intends to surprise you later with a three-hundred foot smokestack. But it has no place in theatre, and tends to raise the price. Drawings should be pictorially clear so that objects and relationships emerge without intense study. At a glance, for example, you should see the proscenium, the apron, the cyclorama—and be oriented quickly.

The electrician may draw some sheets of his own concerning plugging and cable lengths. The important thing, once again, is not to panic. If you want to study a light plot, sit down in good light and trace through just one instrument. You'll see that it really is simple. Everything is there and can be found. Yes, it's a complex forest, but not if you look first at just one tree, then at another. It becomes easier and easier.

Another page worth describing is the lighting designer's quick reference sheet, often written during the last coffee break before setting cues and levels. Some designers write out their instruments and circuits (dimmer numbers) in use-related groups: all the sky colors, the acting areas, side lighting, special effects, etc. Some draw a plan or picture of the stage and jot in the identifying numbers where the light will hit. Some designers use their plot or instrument schedule sheets just as they exist. The purpose is to guide the designer easily when calling out levels to the board operators. When you want to dim the refrigerator light one point, you must find that circuit (dimmer) number quickly. I've known designers who are sensible enough to plan this part of the work well in advance, but we all hate a show-off.

"Several times, in the past year or so, I have sat at my desk in an upper-floor room facing north on East Sixty-ninth Street, looking straight at the reflections of the sun in one or another window-pane of a tall apartment building on Seventy-second and Third Avenue. The panes where the sun appears, around early afternoon, vary slowly with the season, as you might expect, and much more quickly with the time of day. If I look long enough, I can carry as many as eight yellow-green after-images of the sun, place them wherever I want to on my wall, and move them up or down, all eight suns, at will."

—Lewis Thomas

7 *Control*

Courses or books concerned with stage lighting often begin with a discussion of control—the dimmer board. It is well argued that artistic capabilities are limited by the amount of control and its sophistication. But this could also be another way of saying that you can't be an artist until you've entered the technician's labyrinth and overcome the beast in the center, electricity.

Not so. Control has become simpler, and we usually have enough places to plug our lamps. Deft operation of these dimmers is rarely a problem today. If you haven't enough dimmers for all the instruments you want, you simply apply common sense and set up artistic priorities.

As for electrical theory, we need no deep understanding of that. Cooks don't know the precise scientific explanation of cooking, which is a frightfully complex process of molecular and physical changes of organic compounds under heat. If you are curious about electricity, start with a simple high school text or, as I do, with a good children's encyclopedia.

We've controlled our dramatic light since theatre began. Perhaps it all started when we started moving away from the campfire for scary effects. We began plays so that the sunset would catch us at the right moment. Candlelight could be altered with shields or filters rotated or lowered in front of the flame. Remote turn-downs lowered the gas. When electricity came to us, we promptly started to adjust the strength of its flow to our lamps. Ingenious and shocking methods appeared, such as passing the current through variable depths of salt water.

The basic control unit is the dimmer board, often called the switchboard. This is a group of dimmers, and each dimmer can be dimmed up *(sic)* or down to control the lights plugged into it. Each dimmer has a capacity, which means what capacity always means—it can hold just so much. If you overload it (plug too many lamps into it) a fuse will blow. Capacity is easy. If you have a three-thousand-watt dimmer, it can control three one-

"One memory haunted her more than any other, reminding her of this lonely unknowable feeling in her life. It was when she had been a young mother at twenty-four, she was calling her children to supper from the back porch of the house, shielding her eyes with one cupped hand as the sun was breaking through great frames and knots of grey March clouds at dusk, suddenly sending its magnificent red light down upon everything. She was calling out the names of her children, and her children were abroad in the strange otherworldly red light of late afternoon, abroad in the sighing organ sounds of dusk, calling back to her. And she had paused, uneasy, standing there on the porch in that strange red light, and she had wondered who she really was, and who these children were who called back to her, and what this earth of the strange sad light could be."

—Jack Kerouac

thousand-watt lamps. Simple as that. Or it can control six five-hundred-watt lamps—or four seven-hundred-and-fifty-watt lamps. Did you panic here for a moment? Silly—it's as easy as making change.

Here's description of the dimmers on three kinds of dimmer boards: The Resistance Board, The Autotransformer Board, and All the Swell New Boards.

THE RESISTANCE DIMMER, like all dimmers, hopes to supply your lamp with no electricity if the handle is all the way down, and with full electricity, and therefore full brightness, when the handle is all the way up. It tries to do this smoothly—a steady build or wane between these extremes.

The resistance dimmer is a creature you may never meet, but join me here in a moment of respect. Each dimmer was called a plate, and looked like a huge poker chip or a small manhole cover. A handle pivoted from its center. In these plates, coils of wire were baked into insulating porcelain. These wires resisted current, impeded its progress. This turned the current into heat energy, like the glowing wires in your toaster. The rotating handle had a shoe (sliding contact) which slid around the edge of the plate, contacting little brass buttons. These buttons were the points at which the coiled wires came out for air, and as you raised the handle, the buttons you contacted represented less and less coil inside, therefore the current ran through fewer toasters and emerged less impeded, stronger and stronger, until the top button where there was no handicap and it ran full strength.

It worked. It really did. All of its problems could be overcome, and clever groupings of the plates and mechanical connections between the control handles could move a dozen dimmers by heaving just one handle. You could also control a lot of small-capacity dimmers by plugging them all into one big one. Dimming up the big one (called the master) turned them on to wherever you had pre-set them. If you rented these boards for a show, you could swap different capacity dimmers and arrange them in the board's housing to suit your needs. If you had a big sky, with tons of light hitting it, you might want many six-thousand-watt plates to group all those colors together with the fewest control handles. If you had a lot of bitty things, like table

"In some of these dense fir and spruce woods there is hardly room for the smoke to go up. The trees are a standing night, and every fir and spruce which you fell is a plume plucked from night's raven wing."

—Henry David Thoreau

lamps, you could choose many small-capacity dimmers for them.

This is the board that has to be loaded just right. If you have a three-thousand-watt plate, you must load it with at least two-thousand watts worth of lamps, or it won't dim them out. This is because the lamps become a partner in the toaster business, and this resistance process doesn't work unless there's a load of electrical devices, lamps or toasters, to resist. You can't resist what's not there. Don't try to understand that, but know that if you have a three-thousand-watt plate, and only two five-hundred-watt lamps to plug into it, you can plug in an extra two-thousand-watt lamp, put it backstage out of sight, and the lamps out front will now dim happily, joined by this unseen companion shining inconspicuously in the dressing room toilet. This is called Ghost Loading, and adds to the heat and confusion.

You could repair these old boards yourself, and even drop them off the truck without losing all hope. They seemed like mechanical, if not electrical, marvels, bristling with handles, grooved shafts where cogs clicked in to link the handles, rows of big fuses, and porcelain socket boxes stacked on top. They were cozy in winter and hot as fire in summer, during the long night scenes when the lamps were dim and all the constrained juice turned to heat. You operated them with both hands, both feet, an elbow or two, always knees, and an occasional chin or anything else you could put into action. Fires could be extinguished. With a good kick, a dying board could finish the act. They were lovable and we mourn their passing, and we created all the beauty there was to create and enjoyed the rewards so hard-earned. On the other hand, we could say, with Anton Chekhov, "Strickly speaking, to hell with them!"

AUTOTRANSFORMER DIMMERS take a different tack. Even I learned, in grade school, that if you wind wires around an iron frame, and wind more wire around another piece of iron inside this, the current will pass from one coil to another. (It can also make it spin, like an electric motor.) The point is that by adjusting the relationship of these two non-touching coils, you can adjust the flow of current. This can dim your lamp. You move a handle or turn a dial, change the relationship, and the current

"The sun goes down to rest and the rays of the sun get fainter and fainter and darker and bigger shadows come. They get darker and bigger till it's their period and time. They creep out of the cupboards after being imprisoned. No more is the room welcoming, no more is it inviting. The ticks of the old grandfather clock get louder and louder and like a deep black ink called darkness which devours all light slowly eating its way through the room till there's nothing left but it."

—Timothy, Age 10

is weakened or strengthened—without the physical need to drain off unwanted current as heat. Another advantage of the Autotransformer is that you can dim a small lamp with a big dimmer, and therefore needn't be so picky with lamp grouping. You can make choices more freely, with no ghosts in the toilet.

Another good thing about Autotransformers is that the dimming curve is more reliable. Resistance dimmers have a way of lying in wait for you as you raise the handle. Nothing at one, two—then a burst of light at three. This is like the gas gauge on my Chevrolet, which hangs forever at full, then zooms down to almost empty, and lingers again. It's all the more tiresome when each individual dimmer has its own unlovable eccentricities.

As in Resistance boards, you can feed many small dimmers through one giant one, and this is called electrical mastering. But Autotransformers are still bulky and heavy and need mechanical and even muscular virtuosity. They do come in neat package boards, handy to carry about and install temporarily. They're useful, but fading from the scene.

Today, technology treats us to electronic dimmers with computer controls and computer memories: *All The Swell New Boards*. With the punch of a button one of these boards will memorize whatever is onstage at that moment, and another punch will bring it back any time, and in a twinkling. You can use calculator-style buttons, or neat little handles that move up or down, and you don't need a lot of them. A dozen might be enough, and a few calculator-style buttons will hook these surrogate handles into any circuit or group of circuits you want. When you've adjusted these, you can commit to the machine's memory and move to other circuits and when you've done all you want, you push the right button and Zap! cue twenty-three is ready to go. To go from cue to cue, a little handle is pushed at any speed you want, or it pushes itself, once started, at exactly the speed you've ordered beforehand. If you run your cues out of the usual order, you can alert the system and it will deliver any cue you want, any time. For a twenty-minute sunset, you can relax and let the long timer tick it away.

Of course there is a computer read-out panel that will tell you the level of every circuit in every cue, what cue you're in, what cue is next and how long it will take, and so forth. One that I'm

"We drove up the steep winding road to her house near the top of the Hills. The night was clear and it seemed as if the world was full of nothing but little pulsing lights above us and below us. It was so beautiful you thought you ought to say something about it, but there was nothing good enough to say. I felt as if we were floating between two starry skies, flowing into each other at the horizon."

—Budd Schulberg

using now makes rude remarks. "You're making a mistake," it flashes.

Computer technique is now easy for us—the computers know plain English. To recall cue twenty-six, for example, you might push a button named Q (for cue), then the numbers 2 and 6, then G for "go". If you want to change the level of one circuit, let's say Circuit 43 in Cue 26, you might push one button symbolizing cue, then 26, then one button for circuit, then 4 and 3 for Circuit 43, then 65 (the new intensity level you want on a scale of one to one hundred), etc. The computer display might light up saying, "Are you sure?" because it doesn't want you to change its memory casually or carelessly. But it will give in.

Does this seem like a lot of button pressing? It's not—it moves along quickly and logically.

Another system that has been in use for a long time, and is still fine if you have too small a system or budget for the memory luxury, is the PRE-SET arrangement. You have rows of tiny handles, each handle for a dimmer circuit. If you have ten of these rows, you can set them for your first ten cues. Then, using another handle sometimes called a fader, you can go from cue to cue. If there are twelve cues in the first act, you can re-set the first two rows when you've finished with the first two cues. If you've bought a system with only two pre-set rows, you have to set up the next cues at a lively pace. But if only a few circuits move, you don't have to re-set the whole row, but just push the needed handles.

The dimmers behind the controls of these new boards have undergone great changes and great advances, and have complex names. At this moment, they are called Silicon Controlled Reflectors (SCRS) and they are, basically, clever little switches that switch the current on and off at a great rate. They work with household style alternating current, which is known as sixty-cycle current. To complete sixty cycles, the current changes directions one hundred and twenty times each second. The switch nips into this cycle at each change—one hundred and twenty times per second. That's the trick—the amount of current allowed to pass through this controlling gate depends on exactly when the gate opens. It can open when the current is just turning, just reversing itself, and barely moving; or it can open when the current is at the height of its cycle and in full flood.

Enough of that. You have nothing to fear, nor anyone to regard with awe. If anything, the boards are kinder to the non-technical creator. Also the new boards operate remotely; the little control consoles activate banks of dimmers that are tucked away elsewhere. This means that the mysterious board operator is not always buried backstage linked to the massive toasters, but may be in front in a control room with a view of the stage. The designer and board operator can now sit in the auditorium with the small dimmer board, which looks like any home computer with its keyboard and screen. Or take a tiny device the size of a television control to any place on or near the stage and adjust from there.

Computer control allows us to handle a tremendous number of instruments. When I began lighting, in the fifties, three hundred units was plenty for a musical—there was no room for more than eight or ten big piano boards, and no money for more than the four or five big men to work them. Now, one computer keyboard and one operator control the eight hundred lamps we sometimes have, and the dimmer banks are tucked away in the cellar.

Besides the new wonderful effects, we seem to need half again the brilliance we needed twenty-five years ago, just as we need half again the volume of sound. That's the way it is.

8 *Areas and Angles*

Let's return to what the designer worries about when he or she is making the light plot: building up the total design. We divide the stage into bite-size areas, and this seems simple and logical today. A man who should not be forgotten, Stanley McCandless (a wonderful name for an incandescent pioneer), articulated this system in the thirties, following the initial improvement of focusing spotlights that make it possible. Robert Edmond Jones, Jo Mielziner, and others were also frontline pioneers; but it was McCandless who wrote it down and developed it into a system that was useful for many years, but is old-fashioned now, since it does not give enough meaning to side lights or the sheets of powerful color we can use now.

Before this work, a system of borderlights, footlights, floods, follow spots and the occasional shafts or pools gave us general, even light, and color variation for night, and the occasional punctuation for melodramatic effects.

For ballet or opera we still usually build from washes of color from the front, overhead, and sides. These can be interplayed to give the needed basics, and follow spots, some specials, and some particular areas can produce light on the principals. But in a play we can't escape the idea of areas. We usually build from areas and then add the washes and effects.

An area is a logically grouped set of instruments doing one job on one part of the stage. In a simple interior, one might portion the stage into three areas across downstage (left, center, right) and then do the same upstage. There might be more areas depending on furniture grouping or platforms. The downstage areas will usually be lighted by spots from the front of the house and the upstage area from spots on the first pipe. Each area might have two or more spots from the right, and two or more from the left. If the spots are thoughtfully placed and carefully focused, the light hits an actor from both sides at a good angle so that he or she is well covered.

Areas usually overlap and blend, so that actors can move

"Once we were hove to about 5 miles sw of the Wolf Rock, the wind had died away in a flat calm, the sea like a mirror, very dark without a cloud in the sky and the stars shining in the water the same as in the sky, all the lighthouses showing their lights all around the horizon and the Lizard light flashing in the sky. I . . . started to row back. After pulling for some time I stopped to see if I could pick up the skiff's light but with so many stars in the water I could not find it . . ."

—Peter J. Stuckey

about and seem to be in the same atmosphere stage right as they were stage center, with a smooth transition as they move. Some areas are separated, of course, such as the pool of light on the evening veranda.

One thought: the division into areas drawn on the plan is often shown by slightly overlapping circles. These circles are usually not on the floor but at head height. The light will continue to travel and widen as it nears the floor. We had trouble with this in Japan, where performers are expected to spend more time close to the floor.

In most area concepts, the instruments are plugged so that each area is controlled by a single dimmer handle. Sensibly, this might define areas: if you use two dimmers it might be better to divide the space you light into two areas, and take advantage of this finer-tuned control.

We use the word "angle", and there's a broad hint of good or bad angle. Let's go to basics. A light hitting a face from straight out and low will flatten it and hit the set behind it. The flat-on shot pardons wrinkles but gives no molding to the face, casts a distracting shadow behind it, and makes the set competitive in brightness. If we place a light too steeply overhead, it will cast deep shadows hiding the eyes. This is a bold, dramatic effect for MacHeath on the scaffold, and it is good edging or toning light. Save it for those uses.

Lights from directly left or right leave the far side of the face unlit: again a good device if starkness is in order. From both sides at once, side lights alone would leave the front of the face peaked.

To bring out a face, well-molded, neither stark nor flat, with eyes visible, lights from both sides at about a forty-five degree angle seem best. Some say that the diagonal of a cube is best, and that image shows at least what is meant by "forty-five degrees": the diagonal coming towards the actor from above and half-way between dead ahead and dead abeam.

With most of the stage hit this way, you have your basic stage light: your walk-around areas, perhaps your furniture groupings, a flight of stairs that might be big enough to control as an area, a restaurant table, and so forth. The control is sensible, and you can easily focus the stage picture on the important area at

". . . the maples turn a blazing bitter red, and other leaves turn yellow like a living light, falling about you as you walk the woods, falling about you like small pieces of the sun so that you cannot say where sunlight shakes and flutters on the ground, and where the leaves."

—Thomas Wolfe

any moment if needed. Why does it look like dishwater? There are things left to do.

Color: the good angle on the face isn't enough. You probably need a variation in tones, such as a warmer color from one side, a cooler from the other. This adds modeling—it sculpts the face, making it easy to read—and it can help if some of the available angles are poor.

Side lighting: shots added from the sides fill in behind the ears for those watching from side seats; it can add slightly richer color tones; and it blends the areas because it sweeps across all or most of them. It usually falls off on the sides of the stage and does the least damage to the set. It edges or haloes the actors and pulls them out of the background.

Top light: call it back light if you want. Again, it gives edging and halo to the actor, and can bathe the stage in a general color tone.

Specials give us the emphasis, the extra punch, and the coverage of places too specialized or small to call for a grouping of lamps. We hit the doorways for entrances, the place on the sofa for that long monologue, the pool of extra warmth around the table lamps. That dramatic downlight for MacHeath would be a special, and Candida's firelight or leaf patterns could be called specials, though some prefer to call these "special effects" or "projections."

Some lights could be labeled specials or special areas or, and here's a daring idea, you could just call them what they are, such as French Door Sun Circuit. That suggests a circuit of big units shooting through a door. Your actors can't always bask in those particular shafts, yet you want the feeling throughout the room. Therefore you might add some extra specials from the motivating direction—where the sun is, in this case. Keeping an angle similar to the main shot is important. Side shots might do this, or shots from the end of an overhead pipe.

For night scenes, perhaps the area instruments can be duplicated by other units, focused the same way but colored for night. Or it might be more practical to use a color wash to change the whole stage tonality. The area colors will appear differently against a night background. Perhaps specials can flood in to warm or cool the area even more. Side lights of a

". . . the girl's form remained a vague outline and, peered at through a fire that reached as high as the concrete ceiling, became almost indistinguishable from the wavering flames themselves.

But then the boy happened to blink his eyes, and for an instant the shadow of his lashes, magnified by the firelight, moved across his cheeks."

—Yukio Mishima

different tone can help here. At night we usually look to strong motivating sources, often warm in tone, such as table lamps or streetlights, or cool such as moonlight. You can have strong light on your actors in night scenes: the trick is meticulous planning of angles and a crafty focus to keep your backgrounds dark.

Basic areas, washes, specials. Is that the only way to go about it? Most of what you can do is implied in these generalities, but variations are infinite, and these three types of light are always being redefined. Be awake to new sources, new motivations. Question where the light is coming from and why. Is the sunset hitting everywhere it can? Is it really the right color? Is it any old sunset or the one you want?

The area approach takes certain things for granted. When it was developed, each dimmer handle needed a push up or down, and only logical grouping could physically control a show. Today's miraculous memory boards control every lamp with just one tiny lever elegantly moved by a ninety-eight pound weakling. Therefore you can try other things. But lamps do usually demand grouping: you wouldn't want six hundred individual controls even if you could have them. Perhaps you might use simple washes and specials, each moment caught in its own way, and never submit to the generality of an area. It can work. But there probably will be an area or two, even by some other name.

In musicals today we move tons of wattage, and fast, in great sheets of color. It's possible with the new controls. Area thinking may be outmoded in these cases—principals can be picked out with specials and spots. Increasingly, spectacular light effects are built into the sets, above, behind, and below the performers. Again, new ways must be found to pull out the faces.

Let's come back to angles. From what angles do these fronts, side lights, top or back lights, and specials hit? Where do you mount the units? From the front-of-house, you might have a first balcony rail, and possibly a higher second balcony rail. There could be a ceiling slot or cove, side auditorium slots, or box booms. Follow spots can come in from far up at the back, or from the ceiling slots.

The first balcony rail is a low flat-on shot, but fine for the big light of some dance numbers, fine for some specials, projections

"In the dining hall of the Arrakeen great house, suspensor lamps had been lighted against the early dark. They cast their yellow glows upward onto the black bull's head with its bloody horns, and onto the darkly glistening oil painting of the Old Duke.

Beneath these talismans, white linen shone around the burnished reflections of the Atreides silver, which had been placed in precise arrangements along the great table—little archipelagos of service waiting beside crystal glasses . . ."

—Frank Herbert

and effects. From either end of the balcony, you can shoot in at a nice angle. A second balcony or ceiling cove moves the lamps up closer to that good forty-five degree angle. Even from this angle, you might not shoot straight in, but divide your lamps to hit actors from both left and right. The light will model the faces, and its bounce will be to the side, instead of on the background.

The side slots or box booms are favorites for basic actor light. They are close for punch, and the fall-off or bounce light is to the side. When focusing these, the top lamps might hit the far side of the stage, the middle the center, and the low lamps the near side. This keeps the angles of these beams as close to parallel as possible so that an actor doesn't age ten years as he or she steps from one beam into the next. Getting into refinements which are not mysterious, just meticulous, a designer might choose lenses that are narrow beams for the long shots and wide for the short shots. Further adjustments of wattage and color might keep the long shot and the short shot in nice balance if they must be plugged into the same control circuit.

On stage, the first pipe is usually the basic mounting position for hitting upstage actors. We try to keep the angles reasonably consistent with front-of-house units, so that an actor walking upstage stays in similar light. Again, we usually pair from left and right on our basic areas, and we overlap to avoid jumpy transitions when the actor moves.

Side light often comes on stage through slots downstage, between the proscenium and the set. If there are no side walls to the set, but open wings, there can be side light galore. If there are walls and a ceiling, and the set is so deep that you can't reach upstage from the first pipe, you might sneak in upstage shots through slots behind a bookcase, pilaster, or potted plant, with help from the set designer. Sometimes a beamed ceiling or a chandelier rosette can mask a hole for a helpful ray.

An open stage without a ceiling may call for many light pipes, permitting thick down light and a lovely choice of angles for specials. Down light or back light needn't be blocked by a ceiling if there is a skylight, a bombhole, etc. But if it is blocked, hope for good side shots.

Specials can be for dramatic statements, such as a shaft of

light. If they are to reinforce an area, or to highlight a door for entrances, there should be thought on the consistency of angle with other instruments hitting that area, so that an actor can move smoothly out of the special into the surrounding light.

All of this is over-simplified, glib and general. But it illustrates how we light in a logical build-up from basics, just as we act or direct or do anything else. Needs can be thought of one at a time, and they can be questioned and understood. There is nothing terrifying in the process. The complexities break down into definable and separable detail. Good ideas are usually not complex anyway. Just relax and have them. Go back to chapter One. Look again at what Robert Edmond Jones said.

9 Levels and Cues

We say that we set cues. What we really set are levels or, as the old-timers say, we "balance". A cue is the *movement* from one setting of levels to the next. We say that we are in cue twelve after we've completed cue twelve—and before we start cue thirteen. But it's not important, and any way you say it, it will be clear enough.

Cues—the pace and orchestration of the shifting light—can be a powerful aid to the play. Do we want the audience to ponder a certain line? Should we therefore leave a glow on that actor's face as we fade? But is it the actor pondering the line, or the audience? Perhaps a simple pause before the next scene, without featuring the actor, is best. Or does energy and content demand a quick pickup on new entrants even as the old scene fades? The shift of lighting directs attention, particularly on open stages where you must move whole heads, not just eyes. Cues can start slowly, then pick up speed and slam to a finish, or the reverse. One important key light can move more quickly through a low change. Think in actors' terms: they must know if they're just leaving the stage, or if they're going to another room.

Never think of a cue as a mere change from one setting to another. No matter how fast the change, a motive or even a convention lurks in it, and that should be in your thinking as you work out the pace and organization of the shift. With old boards, the operators couldn't always handle everything at once, and shrewd routing was part of the fun. Today it's so easy that often we don't set priorities and our cues may lack inner texture.

Never let your stage become ugly or drab through carelessness. An old saying tells us to lead in with the cools and lag out with the cools—"cools first in, last out". Perhaps. This keeps away that brown stain of low-level filaments. It's worth a thought as you go along.

Again, the answers are easy if you just keep asking the ques-

"Guenever was singing and brushing, her low voice fitting the stillness of the candles."

—T.H. White

tions. When exactly do the table lamps in a room go on or off? Do they merely get homogenized in with the rest of the moving light, or do they lead it or lag it? Do they snap on to precipitate an exact moment when the room is established? Do you want to lead in with locale and/or mood-setting devices such as a moment of stained glass shafts or Venetian blind stripes before the full light pales them?

We're running ahead of ourselves: we've just moved light we haven't set. We've rechecked our circuits, now focused, and carefully, one at a time. It's clean now, each circuit (area, special, tone or wash) ready to do its job. But just as you will, I've nervously delayed the scary moment when we finally sit down facing the dark stage. There's the plank for a desk, teetering on seat backs. A table lamp or clip-on light, probably too dim to reveal the paperwork, suddenly seems blinding when the stage must be seen. The intercom is probably rotten—a good reprieve; we can waste some time getting comprehensible speech to come out of both ends of that. It's all as frightening as sitting in front of a blank piece of paper, but a start must be made—somehow. Start by accident if necessary, but start. Perhaps someone's been appointed to walk the stage, to give us a target to see our levels and angles. Out of simple consideration for safety, get some light on stage.[1]

Incidentally, let the lighting designer possess that plywood island. Stay near if you're wanted, but don't foul it with your styrofoam cups, your raincoat and morning paper. Also keep the designer's aisle free—he or she will want to move out quickly to check the job from other places in the auditorium.

If there's sky or a surrounding space that needs lighting, that could be your start. Don't fiddle with it forever, because it will need adjusting when acting light starts bouncing into it. Perhaps you want to be stingy at first: don't pile on everything and leave nowhere to go. Some designers will make a fast and seemingly final decision, others like to sketch it first, the way we can

---

[1] When I was an apprentice in London I worked for a designer who could not face a clean crisp sheet of white drawing paper. One of my tasks was to take a new pad and go through it page by page: a wrinkle here, a smudge there.

"Moon Orchid laughed softly in delight. 'And look here. Look here,' she said. She was holding up a paper warrior-saint, and he was all intricacies and light. A Communist had cut a wisp of black paper into a hero with sleeves like butterflies' wings and with tassels and flags, which fluttered when you breathed on him. 'Did someone really cut this out by hand?' the children kept asking. 'Really?' The eyebrows and moustache, the fierce wrinkles between the eyes, the face, all were the merest black webs. His open hand had been cut out finger by finger. Through the spaces you could see light and the room and each other."

—Maxine Hong Kingston

rough in an acting scene. There will be time to adjust, in any case.

After the sky, perhaps you'll come downstage. Add some color toning from downlights if you have them. Now start something for the actors: areas, then side light. Readjust the background. Now garnish with specials and check the acting moves. Is this now your first moment? Should you slip in some of your following needs so that a second cue isn't called for right away? Or do you prefer to have the light growing in these first moments?

Don't fall to the temptation of a serve-all level that may miss the subtle movements in feeling. The most ordinary space looks different to us as we shift concentration. Subtle movement of specials, of this and that area, can reinforce the composition and therefore the thought. Or would that be too fussy for a straightforward play that doesn't need constant dickering? A lot depends on the set: does it pull your eye to the right when your actors are to the left? How much can we help this problem with lighting? And never bore us by saying (as Hamlet hefts a grapefruit instead of Yorick's skull), "If they're going to be bothered by that little thing, we're in real trouble." If you work that way you're the one who's in trouble.

Let's start all over. Perhaps it's a simple room on a sunny morning. Without regretting it, your designer might slam on the sun that blasts through the window. He might start it at full, because this shot is rarely too hot. I'd start it at nine (out of ten) just from superstition, remembering the old saw that if all your handles are up, you haven't got enough light. In other words, you should have enough units and a clean enough focus for elbow room even in your brightest scenes. Here, in our simple room, we probably won't light the scenery at all. Bounce, probably far too much, will do that for us. (Ceilings are so often painted too light—it's amazing how dark they can be and seem right.) Continue now: try areas and side balance. Again, the same questions. Is this just the first moment? Some specials. Is the door special critical for a first entrance? Is an actor at the window and sun-edged? Arty? Is the stage spotty? Is that good for these moments? Even if your actors should move in dim

". . . your limbs fell off by themselves when I tried to hold you in my arms because they had removed the innards of everything that held together your live body of a sleeping happy mother with her hand on her heart and they had stuffed you up again with rags so that all that was left of what had been you was only a shell with dusty stuffing that crumbled just by being lifted in the phosphorescent air of your firefly bones and all that could be heard were the flea leaps of the glass eyes on the pavement of the dusk-lighted church . . ."

—Gabriel Garcia Marquez

light until they reach key positions, is it rich dim light, or just thin soup?

When the actors step upstage, is the light from the first pipe different from the light they enjoyed from out front? Why? Just a dimmer adjustment to match the intensity of the first pipe lamps with the more distant front spots? Have you focused badly, and a whole new breed of light is hitting upstage, with different angles and different colors? Are the side lights blending the transition or emphasizing its faults?

If you're the director, keep looking, noticing, helping at the right moments. This is the lighting designer's hardest job, looking objectively at work he or she has created, the same problem that directors, actors, playwrights, and producers all share: never lose touch with what you are trying to achieve. For example: virtuous as it is, just plain good visibility is not enough for a professional. How is the character being shown to us? By what light—moonlight, starlight, office light, artificial stage light?

Do you emphasize a dramatic moment by a different angle of light? Even in realistic motivation, places can be found that create a special image. I remember a minister who was present at a rural gathering, and moved about to stand in the heavenly shafts of light coming through the broken barn roof.

Is there a moment when you want to emphasize hands? Shroud eyes? Does a special angle, a place, seem to pull a character into himself or herself? Does a glowing table lamp make a room brighter, or underline isolation? Does it emphasize light in the room or growing darkness outside the room? Can you bring a chill of foreboding with light the way you can with creepy music in films? Can the set designer help place objects that cast shadows?

Take a good look at colors. Will a face be moulded more if there is greater differentiation in tone on one side? Do the faces seem cleanly lighted? Are there a dozen different colored shadows under each chin?

Do the forms come forward from the background? In sets without ceilings, downlight can etch the edges, but side light can do this too. Is there too much light on the background? Do the figures glare, and more light doesn't help?

What about an opera, with few worries about the diva, who

"Waves dancing joyously across Massachusetts Bay met the sloop coming out, to dash themselves instantly into myriads of sparkling gems that hung about her breast at every surge. The day was perfect, the sunlight clear and strong. Every particle of water thrown into the air became a gem, and the *Spray* making good her name as she dashed ahead, snatched necklace after necklace from the sea, and as often threw them away."

—Captain Joshua Slocum

has two follow spots. The chorus looks pretty because the tones of light bring out the costume colors. But do the color, focus, and intensity show you spotty pools of color, or a blend? How does it compose? Should you re-block? What's really wrong?

Look at the chorus of a ballet. Do you see only legs? Fat legs? Maybe too much edging from both sides, with the halos widening the profiles. Maybe they *are* fat and it's not our fault. Help them anyway. Take down the light from one side. Ease down front light—then try it higher. Adjust the background. Is the light too hot?

You started with a firelight flicker as Candida and Marchbanks began their scene. Now it's all you see and you can't hear the words. You should have asked to ease it out sooner or, more likely, brought up the area and specials sooner. We've all gotten the firelight message and it will stick in our consciousness as the scene progresses. There can still be motivation from that direction—non-flickering, we hope. Thank goodness your set designer had the wit to mask the effect so that we don't now sit transfixed by a mechanical device rotating around crumpled orange plastic.

As director, keep your designer at work and keep the attention where you want it, but don't fuss him or her with ten too-tiny cues a minute and don't ask for your work to be repaired if you've messed up the picture. You may have to move your actors about: the sun shaft can't shift constantly if that's the effect you want. Your designer can help the play, and should feel the mission, but that's different from patching it up. The desperate cry for funnier lights is still in any designer's darker memories.

In a musical, you may sneak light down just a hair so that you can surge up at the end of a number to call for applause. Just how to do this varies with each song and number, like the delicate touch on the follow spot. Once there was a curious offpitch voice and we couldn't locate the yellowbird. It was the electrician, belting out the last bars so that he could get just the right timing and feel on the dimmer handles.

Let's go back again. It's an open stage and you want light, a pre-set, as the audience enters and waits. Or perhaps it's a proscenium stage and, right in fashion, you want to see the stage

"The film of evening light made the red earth lucent, so that its dimensions were deepened, so that a stone, a post, a building had greater depth and more solidity than in the daytime light; and these objects were curiously more individual—a post was more essentially a post, set off from the earth it stood in and the field of corn it stood out against. All plants were individuals, not the mass of crop; and the ragged willow tree was itself, standing free of all other willow trees. The earth contributed a light to the evening. The front of the gray, paintless house, facing the west, was luminous as the moon is. The gray dusty truck, in the yard before the door, stood out magically in this light, in the over-drawn perspective of a stereopticon."

—John Steinbeck

and set before the show starts. Ask questions. What do you want to see? Do you want your audience to get familiar with a complex set so that early and important plot material gets their full attention? Is there a surprise so that they are fooled into this familiarity and then you shift as the show begins? Perhaps you only want a handsome or evocative picture, building their mood.

At the starting moment, do you just go black and then bring up the same set and light again? Does this make the whole idea of a pre-set seem false, or boring? Just when, in relation to all of this, do you dim the house lights? How fast? Smoothly or with pauses? Does the light grow as the actors enter?

Let's go back again. You have your first cue on a simple set. It uses stage spots and front-of-house spots. That's the way you want it to look when the curtain rises. Therefore, you probably want to subtract the front-of-house from the cue, so that the pattern of circles or shutters won't stain the curtain as the house dims. The electrician and designer will agree on a labeling for these initial cues. Perhaps the onstage units are called "pre-set", and before curtain the stage manager will call for the pre-set. Then he'll warn curtain (both the cloth curtain and the electrical curtain cue), and call for the curtain up and the fronts on as it rises. The timing, the interlock of feeling, and the exact way these cues are named or numbered or called can vary. If the board operator can see the curtain, he might take it himself. The reverse of all this might happen when the curtain falls.

When is all this decided? Obviously, all this happens after focus, and after the circuit by circuit check which conditionally confirms your focus. Usually it starts immediately after that check, or after the lunch or coffee break following that check. We can have a separate light rehearsal, with stand-ins to walk the stage. Some shows demand this. Others may not. There are always many interruptions in a technical rehearsal or even in a tech-dress. After spending hours on the lighting itself, you now sit with nothing to do as a hem is pinned or a sound cue repeated. Perhaps you're busy all over again because it just isn't the same now, with full costumes and the set further along. Perhaps those hours of dry cuing, expensive if the set had to be shifted just for lighting, were a waste. If your bookkeeping can keep pace, you might have waited until now, and saved a whole step of time and cost. It's a thought. It depends on the director's ability to give some attention to lights at this moment, and to other factors different for each show.

Sometimes your designer will write out cues in advance, with the confidence of a deaf Beethoven. He or she might have a general list, and call out "Cue Seven, the following circuits to half: 2, 3, 6, 7; now these to three-quarters: 9, 11, 16." Then the adjustments can come. It sounds mechanical, but for some it can save effort and keep the eye keen. That's the important point. The eye must be kept fresh, and the sense of the literature, even in these trying times, must be kept alive.

Rest your eyes when you can. They tire, and you're not always aware of that. They become jaded and everything looks the same, and you're even less aware of that. Your last cues can look like a stale grab-bag of all the left-overs on the dimmer-board. I'd rather push it, and come back, than draw it out. A rush gives roughness, and that needs to be smoothed. A drawn-out session that leads to polished dullness may be almost impossible to repair. Keep your mind moving. Don't think so much about light that you forget what your playwright and actors are trying to do.

IO Cue Sheet and Tracking Sheet

If the keeper of the cue sheet uses a non-smudgy eraser and has clear handwriting, it's not easy to make a mess out of this. A cue sheet might tell us that in cue seven, certain circuits go to certain readings in so many counts (a "count" is usually one second). With the addition of little arrows, we might even see that circuit three goes *up* to six (or sixty) and circuit eight *down* to four. Knowing this direction of movement is vital to the old boards, where manual control requires grouping of the ups and the downs, and two operators rehearsed the way four-handed piano players practise the crossovers.

The new boards make it easy. Perhaps the cue is set up on a pre-set; we then push only one lever to execute that cue. We need the cue sheets only to arrange the pre-sets. If you have a memory board, on the other hand, it will do all of this, and usually have a read-out so that you can see what it's remembering, and what it will remember next. But the old-fashioned cue sheets help if you tour the show and have to re-set on strange boards, or if the computer works no better than my bank's. They also help you plan cue changes between work calls, when you might not have access to the board.

If you have a board without a memory or print-out, a certain thing can happen to complicate the work. Say you are in cue sixty, and suddenly must go back to the moment when she enters with the stuffed cabbage. That was cue forty-one. In cue forty-one, only one handle moved; circuit twenty went up to nine. Wonderful! But what else was on? Well, in the cue before, cue forty, two circuits moved, so they must still be right there, and in cue thirty-nine, six circuits moved—no—one of them moved again in cue forty—let's see—in the cue before . . . The electrician doesn't have time to write down all the handles that *don't* move.

In short, you might have to go back to the top of the act, or some fortunately-placed blackout, and start all over. The solution? A secretary with a tracking sheet. That is a chart sort of

"It was full evening, and the sun within an hour of its setting, the air much warmer now and the light mellow with a powdery gold . . ."

—Hilaire Belloc

thing. Perhaps circuits are listed down the side. The cues are numbered across the top. When any circuit is moved, its new resting place is noted in the little box where the circuit number and the cue number intersect. To go back, you see which handles moved in that cue, then you can glance through the boxes to the left and find the last resting place of every handle. The eye must jerk about as it scans, but with fifteen seconds' practice, you can read off the board at any moment, and as fast as the operators can re-set it.

There is more to the tracking sheet or the computer printout. They can be studied at leisure, and circuits that you forgot to use can be discovered and their fates determined. Circuits that always work together might be combined. Circuits that work rarely, and badly at that, might be axed. Circuits that turn on but never move might be put on a hot-pocket and save precious dimmers, if you're a few short. And when you re-plan, to take your hit on the road, your tracking sheet guides you to the minimum of equipment needed and its most efficient operation.

Good bookkeeping can reveal the small things that cause the big things. In the original (American) *Long Day's Journey Into Night,* so brilliantly lighted by Tharon Musser, a light snapped on in the inner parlor as Mrs. Tyrone passed through, just before she entered to join the dozing men in the main room. The audience gasped at the sudden, unexpected blaze. But at our next out-of-town stop, the audience didn't gasp—they buzzed and murmured. Why? We all scratched our heads. What had changed? Good bookkeeping turned it up. In a change almost too routine to remember, during the move, the small lamp in a hot pocket that snapped on in Boston had been changed to a larger wattage lamp that now bumped up on dimmer in New Haven. The difference? Almost imperceptible, but the snap of a small lamp *struck* the audience—the fast bring-up of a slower-heating large filament *was noticed* by the audience.

While we're speaking of this inner parlor (the little-used formal parlor of the house, as we conceived it), an interesting problem came up. It was to be an unlighted room, dark even at mid-day. How to do this? It was difficult. At first it seemed not lighted—as if the designer had forgotten it—instead of being the part of the lighting design signifying darkness, mustiness. Our solution was to open the drapes a half inch, and let a streak of sunlight cut through the dusty air. This contrast dramatized a room closed off from sunlight. This first impression carried the message through the rest of the play.

I I *The Eye*

The eye itself is an excellent subject for investigation, but other texts can carry you more firmly into this subject, and explain the parts of the eye such as the retina, the iris, the pupil and, not to be overlooked, the connection to the brain. The eye should be aided with spectacles when necessary, and not used for judgments when overtired. It cannot tell subtle differences when used too long. We forget this, and treat the eye as if it is automatically in full gear if we are awake: this is not helped by the notion that open eyes are, to most, the very symbol of being awake. Thus seeing, like breathing, is taken for granted. But breathing is not taken for granted by athletes or oboists, and there is food for thought in this. Not to rest one's eyes at every possible moment, between lamps when focusing or while waiting when setting levels, would be similar to football players racing around between plays in order to stay out of breath.

For those dissatisfied with the technical reach of the above, the following scientific passage from Lewis Carroll's *Sylvie and Bruno* should help.

"And isn't it strange," said the young lady, passing with startling suddenness from Sentiment to Science, "that the mere impact of certain colored rays upon the Retina should give us such exquisite pleasure?"

"You have studied Physiology, then?" a certain young Doctor courteously inquired.

"Oh *yes!* Isn't it a *sweet* Science?"

Arthur slightly smiled. "It seems a paradox, does it not," he went on, "that the image formed on the Retina should be inverted?"

"It *is* puzzling," she candidly admitted. "Why is it we do not *see* things upside-down?"

"You have never heard the Theory, then, that the *Brain* also is inverted?"[1]

---

[1]Lewis Carroll, *Sylvie and Bruno,* chapter XVII.

"By degrees we beheld the infinite Abyss, fiery as the smoke of a burning city; beneath us, at an immense distance, was the sun, black but shining . . ."

—William Blake

During an enjoyable twenty-year period of my life I taught students of college age: aspiring directors, playwrights, producers, critics, and actors—exactly the group I'm addressing in this book. The students designed plays, ballets, or monuments, with emphasis on their interpretation of the script or purpose, not on slick rendering. But we also drew, because of my conviction that serious theatre people must be keen observers. To develop a sharp eye, you must learn to look, not just glance. As Yogi Berra said, "You can observe a lot by watching."

Don't take seeing for granted. It's a developed sense. Foreign languages seem, at first, to be just blurs of tone. You can barely pick out separate sounds until you have clues to the code. Why do you assume that sight is different? An orchestra conductor reads sixteen threads of tone at once, and should be able to detect one instrument that is off key when eighty-five others are playing. I can't hear that, but I might be able to if I'd worked as hard at hearing as I've worked at seeing. Do you have the arrogance to say that your eye needs no such training? How many tones of brown and gray can you perceive quickly in a winter wood at dusk?

And so we drew. Not to become a Degas, but to learn to see. Do this. Take a life drawing class. Join the artists of all time who have struggled with the greatest of subjects, the nude human body. You'll be amazed at the dignity of our shape when you must portray it. Its very familiarity forms the challenge. You will also understand that what we know interferes with what we actually see.

For example: beginners usually draw a neck only because they know it's there. It connects the head to the body at about the shoulders. But stand in front of your bathroom mirror and look down at the faucets, bowing your head comfortably. Without moving your head, strain your eyeballs upward to see your reflection. Do you see a neck? Not a trace. Your head appears to be buried between your shoulders. Your chin is three inches below your shoulder line, which in turn is almost up to the bottom of your ears. Can you believe that three out of four students will, at first, try to show a neck when drawing a pose of this kind?

Next, put your hands on your knees and raise your head to

"Then he saw the bear. It did not emerge, appear: it was just there, immobile, fixed in the green and windless noon's hot dappling, not as big as he had dreamed it but as big as he had expected, bigger, dimensionless against the dappled obscurity, looking at him. Then it moved. It crossed the glade without haste, walking for an instant into the sun's full glare and out of it, and stopped again and looked back at him across one shoulder. Then it was gone. It didn't walk into the woods. It faded, sank back into the wilderness without motion as he had watched a fish, a huge old bass, sink back into the dark depths of its pool and vanish without even any movement of its fins."

—William Faulkner

look straight into a mirror. Your head, as you know, is a relatively small ball on top of your body. But in the mirror now, flattened out, the distance from your chin to the top of your head is greater than the long stretch from your chin down to your navel and beyond. Few students draw it this way at first. It can't really be that way, they reason. It's only because of the foreshortening. Wrong! It really is that way in the mirror, and it really is that way on the flat paper you'll draw on. Start to see with the eyes of the painter or draughtsman and understand what the flat paper will accept.

We did many exercises, and here is my favorite. We drew the model as if she were silhouetted on a window shade. We drew just the outline of the form. Then we'd draw the same pose again, but not drawing the outer edge of her solid form; instead we drew the inner edge of the surrounding space, as if she were the last piece missing from a jigsaw puzzle. It's the same line, but seen differently, with a different attack by the eye and, often, far different results from the students.

I often took my classes to a yellow room that had a wall of modern casement windows and a door with a glass panel. Outside was a stone wall, a tree, a sky, and the ocean with its horizon. This is what they described in words and what they drew. Then I would ask them to look for all the squares and rectangles—to concentrate on those elements, and with an *Aha!* and a squinted eye, each would become Piet Mondrian and start to draw squares cut into rectangles cut across by longer and shorter rectangles, composing and relating well. They perceived edging and moldings and square-cut stones that they hadn't ever seen before, and suddenly they felt like artists.

Extend this thought. I asked the class to see rectangles, and they did. I could ask them to look at all the different tones of yellow on that wall, and they'd see ten where a moment before they'd seen one. Then I asked them to see the wall as a child would see it, then: as a kidnapped child held captive. Suddenly the balance would change between the inside space and the outside tree and sky. There is no *one* perception, no *one* objective view, and seeing clearly does not imply this. It means that you can understand and adjust your point of view, dramatize it, use it for theatre.

"He walked down the long white corridor, which led to Athena's room. It had on his left hand a row of old portraits of ladies, and on the right a row of tall windows. The floor was laid with black and white marble tiles, and the whole place looked seriously at him in the nocturnal light. He heard his own footfall, fatal to others and to himself. He looked out of one of the windows as he passed it. The moon stood high in the heavens, clear and cold, but the trees of the park and the lawns lay in a silvery mist. There outside was the whole noble blue universe, full of things, in which the earth swam onward amongst thousands of stars, some near and others far away. O world, he thought, O rich world. . . .

He had come to the door. He turned the handle, and went in. Of all the memories which afterwards Boris carried with him from this night, the memory of the transition from the coloring and light of the corridor to that of the room was the longest lasting.

The Prioress's state guest room was large and square, with windows, upon which the curtains were now drawn, on the two walls. The whole room was hung with rose silks, and in the depths of it the crimson draperies of the four-poster bed glowed in the shade. There were two pink-globed lamps, solicitously lighted by the Prioress's maid. The floor had a wine-colored carpet with roses in it, which, near the lamps, seemed to be drinking in the light, and farther from them looked like pools of dark crimson into which one would not like to walk."

—Isak Dinesen

The moral of the yellow wall is simply that what you see is changed by what you look for, and what you look for is changed by the increasing vocabulary of what you see sharply. Then you start to see relationships, and you start to design. You must understand that all of these concepts we've been talking about don't appear full-grown in the brain, to be copied down on paper. The pencil point can lead the brain—they work with each other.

More. Yes, the skies are bigger in Holland, for some reason, just as the Dutch landscape painters tell us. And those exaggerated faces—cartoons—by Goya, Rowlandson, Daumier, Grosz, are more real than you thought, when you go to those countries and *look*.

Finally, when you're talking about what you see, be careful of words. They can trigger a stock response and cut off direct sight, just as chosen words can induce perception. Here's a chilling example of the misuse of words and poor teaching. I was the student. My assignment was to render a costume for Iago, and my active mind conceived of this character as a cold and rational villain who pulls down the simpler man of passion, Othello. Ice blue, obviously, would be perfect to cloak Iago, and this I did.

The Master held my drawing up for class inspection, and he was a master indeed, for even at that tender age I let no mere schlimazel wound me deeply. "What kind of a student," he said to the terrified class—and these words alone were enough to shatter my costume career, even before the verb—"what kind of a student would dress Iago in baby blue?"

Don't create solely with words, as I did, and don't destroy with words, as my teacher did. "Bring on the basketball backboards" (all laugh) were the producers' instructions to the Stratford, Connecticut prop crew, and the unfinished frames of Oberon and Titania's canopies came on stage. In the rising mirth the clear and lovely image in my mind of these pieces, handsomely dressed with lace and garlands, cross faded with accurate prophecy to a picture of bent tubing in the back of the truck, on the way to the dump.

Moral: Never show a fool a half-finished piece of work.
Moral: Look hard. Practise. See.

"All the excited couples round us clapped, stamped, cried out and urged the exhausted orchestra to play 'Yearning' over again. And now a feeling that it was morning fell upon us all. We saw the ashen light behind the curtains."

—Hermann Hesse

I2 *Concept*

Concept can be a frightening word. I'll try to explain it, or at least to ease the fear.

Studying a play, one develops a concept for the lighting as well as for the direction and hopefully everything else. The "spine" of a play or scene has been well described by Elia Kazan and others, and that reading is worthwhile and relevant to every aspect of theatre.

An actor studies a part and invests each moment of the character with some image, some objective. These elements may change as the task matures—they may change totally—but they are important from the start, giving fiber to the growth.

A lighting concept isn't always apparent stage center with bells on. Design, after all (the brilliant costume designer Patricia Zipprodt is helping us here), is a combination of perceptions and choices. A concept can be the thread of thought that helps us to choose, that helps us to discard the irrelevant in the act of theatre, which is an act of compression and focus.

Patricia recalls a ballet she designed for Anthony Tudor. Fading leaves was the theme; a metaphor, of course, for the passing of time and lost love. (There are other great themes in art, but when I think of this one, all the others escape me.) Pat's costumes had their vibrant colors high on the body, fading as they went down the torso, down the legs. Each couple was in a different rose palette, against the set's greens.

This idea didn't make the costumes good or bad—a good concept doesn't necessarily create quality. It chooses the arena in which you can excel or fail. Imagine going to a stadium and seeing the field marked out, white lines on the green grass, for football and baseball and tennis, all overlapping. Hard to play the game. What game? It would remind us of so many evenings in the theatre.

Artistic endeavors (this is not an attempt at a definition) deal with a clear establishment of these lines or boundaries or frames, letting them be known, and then pushing and straining

"Perhaps seventy yards to their right was a watchtower; the beam of its searchlight played along the strip. The thin rain hung in the air, so that the light from the arc lamps was sallow and chalky, screening the world beyond."

—John le Carré

at them. This can be misunderstood and, if you don't know it already, you should learn the story of the little old lady who went to an evening of Beethoven string quartets and afterwards rushed backstage to congratulate the performers. "Wonderful, wonderful," she said, "and may your little orchestra grow, and grow, and grow."

A good concept badly executed is an atrocity. Imagine a stadium again. The brilliant green and white gridiron, eighty thousand cheering fans, the yard lines crisply marked—there's your frame. It's dazzling. The teams appear in dirty tee-shirts and bedroom slippers. Do you see what I mean? The game would be better in a back yard.

Let's keep prodding at this word "concept". A lighting concept may seem obvious when a huge transformation is heaped on to a play. "Let's do it as if we've just been swallowed by a whale!" Hold it—is that a concept or just a locale? If the play is *Hay Fever* you've only switched it to a quirky set. Does it really change what happens between the actors? That's what the lighting designer must question. In this whale—are the characters trapped forever? Is there hope—light at the end of the gullet? Is there light only when the whale yawns, and it comes in striped by baleen strips like vertical Venetian blinds? Do we have flashlights with expiring batteries? Does an inrush of phosphorescent organisms supply us with a useful glow?

Silly, but not necessarily so if the play is *Pinnocchio,* where Father Geppetto has come to the end of the world, the pit of despair, the belly of the beast. The symbol of the whale is right and profound. Perhaps his son comes to him as his candle, the shred of his remaining light, is used up and about to flicker out. Now you can get your teeth into it.

I designed a scene for Elia Kazan. The husband comes home unexpectedly one afternoon to find his wife in bed with his best friend. What the director conceived was that at the moment of the husband's entrance the wife was on her way to the bathroom. The apartment entrance door was center, the bed and lover stage left, the bathroom and wife stage right. The set was shallow. Thus the lovers were physically separated by the husband. They couldn't be together. He stood, dividing them powerfully. Her light came from the bathroom, and her face was

"His room was like all the others at Einfried—old-fashioned, simple, and distinguished. The massive chest of drawers was mounted with brass lions' heads; the tall mirror on the wall was not a single surface, but made up of many little panes set in lead. There was no carpet on the polished blue paved floor, the stiff legs of the furniture prolonged themselves on it in clear-cut shadows."

—Thomas Mann

lighted when she turned towards it, away from both men, and dark when she turned to face them. The lover, in bed, was back-lit by the glow of daylight through drawn curtains. (Afternoon love-making has an added wanton and illicit quality.) The husband had the boldest silhouette, from the bright outer hall light and the pale hall wallpaper background.

So, stroke by stroke, we built this striking moment. Of course, as the scene progressed, we brought in enough light to catch all the faces. We wanted to see them clearly. But the quality of the husband's strong position, the dominance and divisiveness we gave him at his entrance, held throughout.

Sometimes the feeling of a painter's light and color becomes the basis of a concept. In *The Tenth Man* we used Rembrandt's ambers and then loaded on yellow backlight through a dusty skylight to halo the performers against the dark golds of the ramshackle synagogue. A sunset at the climax of the play filtered into the room through the skylight again, and the dust and ragged burlap over the glass justified diffusion any way we chose, giving us endless liberty with colors and angles, softness. Then a bash of clean orange light shot across the room when the tenth man himself opened the door. It was the same sunset, and our lighting was wild but consistent and justified.

Ideally the concept covers everything—all the visual effects and the staging. In *No Strings* Joe Layton created such a device. The set and lighting (mine) and Fred Voelpel's clothes joined completely. On one level this musical was about fashion photography. This was the atmosphere in which the principals lived and worked. The sets were movable reflector screens pushed into place by a plentiful supply of live and pretty mannequins. Vast changeable color backgrounds were made from scoops three feet in diameter, faced with deep brilliant color: again, photography devices. Spotlights on wheels were rolled about and operated by the chorus. It was all of a piece, as we say, and its consistency held it together, abstract as it was, for the real emotional contact of the characters.

It had to be strong. In a musical many things happen that can shatter a design. We can create the mood of a scene in a realistic manner, and then dash on a bucket of blazing front light for a dance number, and then yank that up a final notch to call for

"I must explain that we had floated up between the yacht and the launch, whose sailors had passed her a little aside in order to give us room. Her starboard side-light was just behind and above us, pouring its green rays obliquely over the deck of the Dulcibella, while we and the dinghy were in deep shadow between. The most studied calculation could not have secured us more favorable conditions for a moment which I had always dreaded, the meeting of Davies and Dollmann. The former, having shortened his sculls, just sat where he was, half turned towards the yacht and looking up at his enemy. No lineament of his own face could have been visible to the latter while those pitiless green rays— you know their ravaging effect on the human physiognomy— struck full on Dollmann's face. It was my first fair view of it at close quarters, and, secure in my background of gloom, I feasted with a luxury of superstitious abhorrence on the livid smiling mask that for a few moments stooped peering down towards Davies. One of the caprices of the crude light was to obliterate, or at any rate so penetrate, beard and moustache, as to reveal in outline lips and chin, the features in which defects of character are most surely betrayed, especially when your victim smiles."

—Erskine Childers

applause. Then we drop general light and feature our singer in a sharp-edged spotlit circle. We are used to these conventions and they work with the overall scheme if we go back into it with regularity, and if, conversely, there is rhythm and justification to these standard and expected break-outs.

Maybe they're good, these moments that vary a powerful concept. You can get mired in a concept, you know. It can glut, like eating too much chocolate. If I had nothing but moonlight, I'd long for a few fireflies.

One day I visited, as we tend to do, breaking the monotony of a long New York put-on day. Two marvelous designers, Jean Rosenthal (lighting) and Boris Aronsen (sets), were waiting too, sitting patiently in a dark auditorium.

"Don't go near Boris," Jean whispered. "He has a horrible head cold and he's beastly." True, Boris looked like a lump of cow manure with a million green flies buzzing angrily about his head. But it wasn't the body's illness that troubled him most. "I have just seen a production of *King Lear,*" he gasped. "And it was in leather, leather, leather, leather, leather, and leather! As if they had a meeting, got one good idea, and never had another!"

Let's return to *The Tenth Man.* Here, as in *No Strings,* a strong and potentially relentless concept had moments of relief.

The light for the scenes in the young rabbi's cubicle was motivated by the desk lamp. The quality in these scenes was flatter, more ordinary, modern. This made the otherworldly synagogue and its old men even more fantastic when we went back into it with a fresh eye, after a little distance. You can take a sturdy concept and wiggle its tail a bit.

Jean Rosenthal, in *The Magic of Light,* tells us that "you must have the 'flash', the image, the central thread, the idea." All ideas, from the better mousetrap to a lighting concept, eventually gel in a "flash", no matter how little or how much the build-up. But this flash, as she indicates, is a wonderfully broad kind of flash. Suddenly you conceive not merely the idea, but a linkage, a solution, a confident vision of every scene, every problem in the production—all enhanced. You now know how to approach it.

Once I saw a pleasant and rather old-fashioned "drawing-

"Soon the auditorium was filled, and the high-pitched chattering of all the children sounded just like a flock of birds, a level, fluttering, vibrating sound, almost metallic, almost musical. Overhead the earth and the planets moved around the sun. There was a great, soft cry of excitement—the usual response of children to the sudden dark."

—George Dennison

room" play. Indeed, it was set in a New York drawing room. The play was beautifully lighted by Arden Fingerhut. You saw everyone clearly, throughout. In the climactic moment of mock violence the apparent source, the light from a few table lamps, stayed consistent, but fill light dropped out and the moment was just a bit more stark, more dramatic.

Arden chose to keep light coming through the French windows, even at night, which made complete sense to me. New Yorkers living in old houses know that there is usually a streetlight, a security spotlight, or even light from other windows to enter a room. In the play, each time of day had a different glow motivated from outside—soft amber-pink for the mornings, lavender for tea-time, powder-blue at night. The actors moved in slightly warmer versions of each of these tones. Light cast from the table lamps always seemed to hit appropriately, but the overall glow of the pastel light in the Victorian room held sway. Arden also cast subtle projections on the walls, different ones for each scene, web-like soft splinters of light and shadow. All of this, these guiding thoughts, kept it together, and gave her a benchmark for each segment of the play.

A conversation with Arden revealed that she had thought of the house as a place lived in for a long and secluded time, dusty, filled with perfume, and powdery, the way an old woman is powdery. She researched potpourris—dried leaves and spices sold to scent closets and rooms—and found the essence she wanted in rose and lavender. These were the colors she used.

The light from outside was always bluer, whiter, or greener and then was translated into these rose and lavender tones as it reached into the room. The projections were to give a sense of the branches outside in the garden, and these patterns functioned as a device to transform the outside light to a gentle mottling of soft and faded blossoms in the room.

You see above three descriptions of a job of lighting. First, by implication, the general audience's view: good visibility and dramatic moments as needed throughout, a consistent supportive mood in the room, creating the aura, yes, the rose and lavender that is an essence of the old woman who lived there. This sense is there when the curtain goes up. The other characters, two young people, talk and wait—aliens in a gently aged

"The light in the prison, that late in the day, reminded Farragut of some forest he had skied through on a winter afternoon. The perfect diagonal of light was cut by bars as trees would cut the light in some wood, and the largeness and mysteriousness of the place was like the largeness of some forest—some tapestry of knights and unicorns—where a succinct message was promised but where nothing was spoken but the vastness. The slanting and broken light, swimming with dust, was also the dolorous light of churches where a bereft woman with a hidden face stood grieving."

—John Cheever

atmosphere—and then the creator and possessor of the home enters, completing the room physically and emotionally.

Second, more tutored eyes might perceive some of the technique of this, and I described what I saw.

Third, Arden describes her own image, and in this case it is a personal image that was remarkably revealed on stage. The concept was apt and strong, and carried her through the entire play. Other images for other productions ("I thought of steel, its hardness and sharp edges") might be as appropriate, and create as strong a vessel to carry the designer through all the varied seas of a production, whether or not they are finally perceived during the performance.

Concept is many things. A starting point, a generator of ideas, a unifier of ideas. A consistency that nourishes. A color range, a cue or focus system, a painting, a texture. Lighting or costume concepts sometimes take off from the setting concept, but don't just illuminate a set, however strong it may be. Rely on the lighting concept.

The idea, the concept, has arrived when everything in the play seems pulled together, clearer, and all the facets work. When some parts don't fit in, when they strain and you labor and reach to keep your concept glued together—re-think. Don't you patch and glue together a shaky concept. It should glue you together.

One more thought. When we talk about concept, we must consider the glorious word TRANSFORMATION. That's what our work is. We transform our bodies and voices into characters, we transform sunlight into electric light. We look through camera lenses and frame a casually assembled world into a composition, into art.

Now that is why dogs or horses rarely do well on stage. They have not transformed themselves to the same degree as the actors, and a crack appears in the audience's belief. Even inanimate objects must be chosen (and painted etc.) with great care. Some chairs are lively and evocative on stage, some simply don't belong there. A candle is not just a bought thing. With an actor it speaks of loneliness, fragility, hope, loss or impending danger as it is consumed.

And there is no "nothing!" Black drapes are not "nothing",

not neutral. That void can be a most pretentious statement. A bare stage is not "nothing", but another strong statement. No costume is the strongest statement of all—nudity.

We always transform, make the jump. We once needed a colorful tough fabric for tents. What was the most colorful and the toughest available? Tent fabric. Not for us—we used raw silk.

Concept helps, even controls, Transformation. Thinking through Transformation brings on Concept.

I3 *Color*

The unwary take lighting courses to wallow in the glories of color. Sadly, there are few relevant formulae or even solid hints to launch luscious mood adventures.

You know the general theory of light color. The rainbow (first seen, one text hints, by Sir Isaac Newton) starts at violet and goes to blues, greens, yellows, oranges, and to red. These are different wave-lengths, the so-called visible spectrum. The wave-lengths too short to be seen are beyond violet and are called ultra-violet, and there lurk fluorescence and sunburn. At the other end, the wave-lengths beyond red that are too long to see are called infra-red, and relate to heat.

There are three primary colors in light, just as there are in paint, but they are different. This is theory and rarely works perfectly any more than you can expect to get all colors, fresh and bright, from mixing red, blue, and yellow paint. In light, the primaries are red, green, and blue. You get a reasonable yellow if you cast saturated (deep) red light on a face from one instrument, and saturated green on it from another. Yellow is common to both red and green—other colors cancel out. Remember, of course, that the shadow under one side of her nose will be red, and on the other side, green. Remember also that you do not put these two color filters in the path of light from a single instrument: you use two colored beams, and the mix is what is reflected from the surface they hit.

Other mixes are more easily understood: blue on a surface, with red added, will produce purple or violet. Hit with green, a blue will become blue-green. A surface lit with red will become orange if yellow is cast on it, and vice versa of course. Green, a useful color wash, is often discouraged except for special effects. Most of you won't be punished if you use green badly, but my son was when he worked the school follow spot, and chose that color for the principal's speech.

The color of a surface is the color of the light reflected from it back through our eyeglasses to our brain. Daylight, basically

"As they talked about it I noticed that the curtains were open in the living room and there was light coming from the bedroom, also. When they had given me my tea and talked the requisite amount of time they stopped. The whole apartment was silent in light, waiting for me."

—Joanne Greenberg

caused by the sun, has all the colors mixed in it to create "white light". The reflection in these circumstances is accepted as the natural color of the object. When that sun descends, at sunset time, it no longer sends us all the colors, due to filtering out in the atmosphere. All but the red is filtered out in the classic red sunset. Therefore an object has just one color hitting it, and seems to become red. Unless—a big unless—it is painted blue. Blue paint, by definition, is a paint that will absorb all the colors except blue. So it absorbs the red, wanting to reflect blue only. If the red hitting it is pure—if there are no bits of cool bluish or lavender light in this sunset—the object has nothing to reflect and seems to be black. If the object is painted purple, the red beam will find some sympathy, and the reddish aspect of the purple paint will reflect. If the object is green, hit by a red light, it will not become yellow. That's where paint theory and light theory diverge, and on this note we can leave most of this theory behind, because it doesn't help much, and it's not why you've come this far in this text. Stage light is not sunlight but filament or arc light—not pure as the rainbow. For example, pale blue stage light will make red cloth or objects sing out gloriously—certain pale blues, certain fabrics, certain reds.

We don't ordinarily mix saturated colors to make tints useful to the face. Scientific principles aside, the deeply colored filters need wastefully high wattage if adequate light is to reach the stage. We tend to use tints on actors, and save the deep colors for backgrounds or effect light, which can include downlight. Lighting a sky could call for lovely deep color, and if you have a few miles of striplights in a German opera house, you might try the primaries (with a few other things thrown in), and play to your heart's content. In normal and limited work, you might invest most of your limited space and wattage in blues. These need the most punch to read clearly and, in the case of a bright daylight sky, will have the most competition from acting light downstage. Just one circuit of red can usually do what you want: a red sky probably will compete with less bounce from the mood-dimmed actors downstage. Also, due to the warm nature of most filaments, red needs less wattage to show brightly. A red circuit is useful to pull your blues towards violet. The same general thinking could apply to green, which can nicely temper

"Meanwhile the sky circled round, and night fell over the ocean, wrapping in a single darkness the earth, the high heaven, and the treachery of the Greeks."

—Virgil

the blues in a sky. This green, plus the occasional ambers needed, might be achieved with a few scoops. Amber is light and bright, and even a touch will make itself seen. Most of this is generalizing, but it illustrates the thought processes. Usually we know the times of the day we'll need and can gel our lamps accordingly, accommodating the flamboyant sunrise if the need, and the sun, rises.

Mixed into this, as hinted above, is the exact color of the filament. Arcs are cool. Incandescents are warm by nature and push out better through red, yellow, or orange filters. The eye too seems more sensitive to these warms.

The filament is the starting point. It has its color, and its power (wattage). Then the light passes through a lens or lenses, then it goes through a dark or pale gel, then it jumps a certain distance to the stage where it arrives, due to all these matters, weakly or with pep. This arrival is on a reflective or dull surface, light or dark, of paint, nappy fabric, skin with make-up, etc. Other colors usually abound, thrown onstage at other angles. But this is not a deep science for us, just patiently added bits, many of them predictable. It just sounds awful when you analyse it. But there are fewer shifting factors involved than in throwing a forward pass.

Despite the gentle words above, things do seem to get out of hand, so let's pause for a story. We were lighting a scene in which two glorious stars sat on a sofa. Colleen Dewhurst, our lead, looked beautiful and bright, and Lillian Gish, in support, looked beautiful and brighter. The director leaned over and whispered, "David, I love Lillian too, but this is Colleen's scene." We fiddled and focused, and almost doubled the intensity on Miss Dewhurst. No change. Then an idea, and I asked the women to change places. Lillian was so bright we blinked, and Colleen almost disappeared. Obviously, the make-up. Miss Gish was using grease, Colleen the newer products. We laughed, put this to rights, and this helped the playwright win a Pulitzer Prize. Miss Gish taught us something else, learned from the days of cruder light. She had a way of tilting her head just a bit, of lifting her chin just a fraction of an inch, barely noticeable as posture. She glowed in stage light as in every other way—as does Colleen.

"Completely obscured by darkness, the tall figure in black glided to the hallway and down the stairs.

A few minutes later, an almost imperceptible swish sounded as the cloaked being crossed the veranda. People were there, but none saw the mystic personage in their midst. A patch of black flitted across the moon-bathed grass. It was like the shadow of a passing cloud; unnoticed, despite the fact that the sky was cloudless."

—Walter Gibson

Back to filament color. In any incandescent lamp, the filament will burn whiter when white hot, redder when only red hot. Thus down on dimmer, perhaps at one-half or less, the filament may be noticeably warmer. A change will take place in your colors, particularly in the delicate pale blues. If you are using clear light (no color filter), you can play directly with these phenomena. Low level lights, for night scenes, can be appropriately warm, perhaps from an offstage motivator such as a passing tugboat.

Colors, like people, will seem different depending on their companions. Clear will seem warm if the other side of the face is hit by cool, or if the background is cool. Clear light may seem cool if its "surround" is warm. One color, the remarkable "surprise pink", a sort of lavender, has the useful virtue of supplying a real tint but changing its effect in the ways suggested above.

Light usually hits actors from many sides at once. The area light probably comes from the front corners, side light from the sides and only slightly above, and back light from straight overhead. These different shots usually mix on the face, where a slightly warm color, a pale rose-amber, is often desired. But each different color can shine out individually, fleetingly, in little pockets where the others don't reach as the actor moves. This brings fabrics to life. This can be lively, if subtle, or garish—and depends, sadly again, on everything else.

Now is the appropriate moment to avoid harming you with advice concerning exactly what color combinations to use. I've seen this well and modestly done, but to my taste there are too many moving parts for a list. But these are just moving parts, not mysteries. The rules and gel numbers that can intimidate you are spouted from insecurity and territoriality. The good designers just keep searching, and keep extra colors at hand to change to, unashamedly, when things don't work. Yes, they remember the things that work for them the way a chess player remembers the good moves, but the chess player must remember the context in which the moves are relevant. In our case this means the script, the actors themselves, the set, the clothes, the other colors in the air, the size of the theatre and the sightlines. Also, artists tend, sometimes perversely, to search for new com-

"Anna's cut-glass lamp sprang alight over their heads . . ."

—Elizabeth Bowen

binations, and don't enjoy exhuming the same old pieces of surefire business.

Have you ever read advice on exactly what colors to use in a painting? Yes, in the old Lady Books, from which Victorian maidens learned exactly how to draw and color different kinds of foliage and the whole landscape—and at different seasons of the year. This protected them from direct observation, which can be indelicate at times, but it did speed a slick and acceptable product. I had a friend who began his design course by telling his students that straight vertical lines were noble and tragic, and wavy horizontal lines were comic. Red light was anger, blue serenity. He was working on a book explaining how to design and light the ten basic sets when God in his wisdom took him from us, and just before publication. He surely practises in heaven now, where things are done just right, where the primaries are perfect and there's always plenty of punch.

Clichés do work, however, and can be confusing because it's often hard to weed them out of the conventions. It's not easy, for example, to use a night sky other than dark blue. The scenery would have to lead you if you wanted to try that baker's chocolate tone. Sunlight seems to be many different colors, but a pale green needs just the right context to work, and yellow sunlight needs thoughtful treatment so as not to seem a cliché. You may want that pale yellow if it seems to show heat, perhaps more important to a certain scene than the sense of clear brightness.

As in other matters, simplicity should be considered. A sprinkling of many colors in the acting area may only distract and turn muddy when they mix. At other times this may be magical, and some variety is usually good as these colors or tints seek out and reflect from the varied tones, faces, fabrics, and props. A row of downlights or even sky striplights need not have the same colors repeated all the way across: some careful variation may help you towards the vitality that nature itself hands out.

One unfortunate aspect of light is that the "impure" or muted tones such as olive green or indigo aren't a part of the palette. Rarely, by a combination of means, one can achieve the illusion of achieving these colors. Once we ended a Bohème in a soft sepia feeling that was gentle and sad, like an old photograph.

"Sugano pulled up some grass along the path and tied it into something like a broom. To keep fireflies in, he said. There are places famous for fireflies, like Moriyama in Omi, or the outskirts of Gifu, but the fireflies there are protected, saved for important people. No one cares how many you take here. Sugano himself took more than anyone. The two of them, father and son, went boldly to the edge of the water, and Sugano's bunch of grass became a jewelled broom . . . On they walked. It was farther than they had thought. And then they were at Sugano's back gate, everyone with a few captured fireflies, Sachiko and Yukiko with fireflies in their sleeves."

—Junichiro Tanizaki

We worked carefully with the set and clothes, and it didn't always happen perfectly. I think that the sense of slightly furry grey-tan light had something to do with the after-image, so you see how delicately timed the switchboard operation had to be, on top of everything else.

For a practical note, there are three types of color media (color filters). Gelatines (gels) are made from animal gelatine, and are available in the widest range of pretty colors, most of which you'll never use. They are cheaper than other kinds of color, but probably not in a long run, because they pale, burn through, and melt in the rain. A gel placed in front of a hot lens (up-pointing in particular, such as a horizon strip), might pale, then start a small hole which spreads, and the whole thing vanishes in smoke as you watch.

Plastic colors (vinyls, polyesters, or polycarbonates), under trade names such as Cinemoid, Roscolene, Lee, Roscolux, etc., will last longer but not forever. They too love to terrify an audience by smoking for the first minutes of use. They endure rain. But they too will pale, particularly the darker blues. For tough situations, such as the horizon strip noted above, glass can be ordered. It must be pre-cut to size, and is available in few colors, but it is fine if these colors please you and you don't drop them. Plastic and gel come in big sheets which you cut to fit the metal holders which slip into grooves in front of the lenses.

You can double these colors if the tone seems right but pale, or you can put two different ones together to get a perfect third. You can sometimes cut a quarter-size hole in the center. On an ERS this pales the whole tone, and in a fresnel you will get a little blossom of clear tone in the center of the beam, for a face. There are better ways to achieve both of these ends, of course.

What I learned about color was from tiny lamps adapted from toy railroad equipment. I could use the little gel sample books as the color filters, and spent hours of instructive fun. These lamps could be set up on a tiny stage, and we saw the set model and fabric samples under their light. But you must also go to the theatre and see for yourself what works and what fails. Most of you have access to stages and the evidence is reasonably plain— you see the colors at work, and can ask exactly what they are, and what would happen if a darker or lighter or redder or bluer tint had been chosen. Also—to continue our war on mystery—of all things in this book, this is the most available to the perceptive eye. And don't forget to look around you offstage, indoors and out, day and night, where the real things happen.

14 *Crew*

The wise producer or director allows the designers to pick the technical heads, or play a strong role in the decision. This may not be possible in a continuing situation such as a repertory or regional house, but the relationship has to be close, good, and encouraged. Once a master electrician was forced on me by a producer who wanted me watched. A mistake: it was the electrician who was stealing from the producer.

Today crews include specialists that were uncommon twenty years ago. Projections and projection equipment were once the job of the designer and electrician; now this is a specialist's work unless it is simple. The master electrician hangs, plugs, and controls the units, but the sophisticated lensing, cooling, and preparation of slides or film will be the specialist's work.

Sound control has also changed. Rather than simple tapes or records that the electrician flipped on with his nose in passing, we see huge consoles in the auditorium with intricate controls—a total sound mix at hyped volume.

The director's relationship with the lighting crew will be through the designer or stage manager. No real exceptions come to mind. Cordiality is always welcome, for these may be talented men earning more than you. When a director visits during the run, notes on cues that don't work will be given to the stage manager or to the designer, who should visit often to keep the job fresh.

The chief electrician (AKA Master Electrician) is, in Broadway practice, hired at about the start of rehearsal. He or she studies the plot, adds information such as cable lengths, fills out the rental or purchase order, and gets estimates. Work then starts: every instrument is given a physical, the cable is laid out, and special effects are planned, such as smoke or running water (that seems odd, but the tradition grew because turning it on or off is like an electrical cue). Colors are cut, the boards are prepared and pre-labelled.

Assistants were always needed to operate the boards, but

"I dislike him the worse (that is, Schlegel), because he always seems upon the verge of meaning; and lo, he goes down like a sunset, or melts like a rainbow, leaving a rather rich confusion . . ."

—Lord Byron

with new controls a single operator may do, and this is bound to become a fine-fingered speciality, differentiated from the dirty work of overall hang and focus and the old boardside muscle.

If follow spots are used, the chief operator is a skilled specialist. When a show tours, his assistants, who work the other spots, will be hired locally. This chief must give them their cue sheets and rehearse them. A follow spot boss must watch rehearsals and will need time to chat with the director and designer.

On a pre-Broadway tour, the crew chiefs or a manager will phone ahead and order the local crews: so many hands for the put-on, plus an estimate of those needed to run the show. Too many hands waste money and are in each other's way, and too few will miss your deadlines and exhaust everyone. Poorly directed hands waste everything, and this is why good chiefs earn good salaries. Logistics are crucial: what goes up in the air first, how to assemble lights, sets, props and costumes in limited space. Respected chiefs have the clout to get the best local crews and make them hustle.

After the hang and hook-up, one proceeds to focus. This is often the last of the put-on jobs because the set has to be in fair shape before it starts. Therefore, in most cases where union crews are working, the put-on (or "put-in") ends when the focus is done. The unions, with fair reason on their side, usually won't dismiss crews separately: local prop, set, and light crews wait until the show is "on" and then go home, leaving you with your heads and only enough local men to run the rehearsals and performances. You can ask a small ladder crew to come back and touch up instruments if needed. For electricians, your running crew might have board operators, sound operators, follow spot operators, and sometimes a hand to dart out and unplug a table lamp in a quick change.

The temptation is to rush focus and end the big put-on payroll. Within limits this is fair enough, but a sloppy focus will cost dearly when the cast and possibly full orchestra wait for you later. Perhaps you'll rush the last few instruments to finish by midnight instead of five after and save the hour. But at least rush on instruments easy to reach, and plan your focus to leave

"I crossed the staircase landing, and entered the room she indicated. From that room, too, the daylight was completely excluded, and it had an airless smell that was oppressive. A fire had been lately kindled in the damp old fashioned grate, and it was more disposed to go out than to burn up, and the reluctant smoke which hung in the room seemed colder than the clearer air—like our own marsh mist. Certain wintry branches of candles on the high chimney-piece faintly lighted the chamber; or, it would be more expressive to say, faintly troubled its darkness."

—Charles Dickens

them to the last for this reason. Again, within fair limits, this is understood.

If crew chiefs squabble, you're in trouble. One carpenter I hope not to see again became so enraged at the electrician that he actually hopped and then, blind with anger, hung the drops backwards, violating a fairly basic rule of scenery: painted side towards the audience. Another time electricians, who had an easy put-on, refused to handle the hydraulic lifts, which could have been in their jurisdiction. The exhausted carpenters worked three extra days while the electricians and props lolled about, finished. The management paid twenty set-up men for three no-work days.

In stock or regional work, logistics can be easier. Staff and equipment is in the theatre, at work continuously. Most foibles are known. But here protectionism, the "this is how we do it" can be intense. New directors and designers find more resistance than on Broadway, where there is refreshment in the all-new and scar-free start.

Solutions are personal. Asking questions helps. Concealing that you know it all can help. Don't jump too quickly at the conviction that this place is even worse than the last place you worked. The gentle thought that you want some new wrinkle, and the quiet persistent "let's try it" can be an interesting challenge to the most entrenched. Here the producer, who will be re-hiring his crew, can support you by showing a touch of enthusiasm.

Ordinary wiles can prevail. Once I felt that a scenic unit could be tethered by one cable, and only that way would the piece look right and be handled quickly. I knew that the Chief Carpenter wouldn't abide this, so with my heart in my mouth I said, "Sam, you've got the best eye here. One cable might work if *you* put it in exactly the right place.' He leapt to the job. But be careful. Not everyone can be flattered and no one, ever, is quite as stupid as you think.

Don't waste everyone's time with the old complaint that union costs kill theatre. That's a long story, with two sides to it, and an objective breakdown of costs might surprise you. Enjoy working with some of the wisest, most dedicated, most supportive people in the industry.

There is real joy in working on stage with others, a joy rarely matched except in team sports. Sometimes the designer, sometimes the producer, and sometimes the director may be the key person to pull the team together. Keep the big picture in mind, and let everyone know what you see.

15 *Thoughts on Open Stage Lighting*

If you seek one guiding principle of stage lighting, you'll find it in carefully planned and meticulously executed focus. This is the heart of the job. You can jiggle dimmer handles and swap colors to your heart's content. But your lamps must hit where they're needed. Don't rely on leftover light, using the edges of an area or special to fudge into another task. As in woodworking, your tools should be clean and sharp, chosen for the exact job. With the lengths well measured and the corners precise, the assembly—in light that means the levels and cues—is a delight. With a clean focus you can also achieve the hardest of all stage lighting tasks: keeping the light away from where it's not wanted. That's critical to open stages—you can't slop off to the sides.

These thoughts carry us into lighting open stages without a sharp break from proscenium practice. The instruments and the control are the same. The division of the stage into areas arranged for logical control is similar, and so are the specials. The main tools are intact, but there are differences in their use.

Proscenium stages differ in size, shape, and lighting positions, but the general approach remains the same, even though different instruments, lenses, and wattages must be chosen to adapt to different angles and distances. Coming out on to open stages, none of this knowledge is lost, but you must pick it apart to use it on greatly varied configurations. The open stages differ not only in their shapes but in their moods, far more than prosceniums. In open stages the room as a whole is more in our consciousness, and the audience has a different relationship to the stage and the performers in each theatre.

To me, arenas have usually seemed realistic, and three-quarter or thrust stages more poetic. In any case, you must understand these rooms intimately before you can direct, set, or light in them. Usually this is possible—most open stage work is done by artists familiar with the room. When we tour or have casual relationships with a theatre it is more often with a proscenium.

"At last it was the time of late summer, when the house was cool and damp in the morning, and all the light seemed to come through green leaves; but at the first step out of doors the sunshine always laid a warm hand on my shoulder, and the clear, high sky seemed to lift quickly as I looked at it."

—Sarah Orne Jewett

Beware of rooms that cheat. We've created bad thrust stages that have only a token of seating on either side, with little address to these sections from the actors. We've also created thrust stages with fine side seating and few end seats. There is an interesting test if you're directing or lighting in an open stage—do you feel you have to move all around the auditorium to do your job? Is one end, one direction, overweighted?

Side lighting is tricky on an open stage because it blasts into the house unless it has an end or wall to hit. But what is the side, anyway? We're seeing our actors from three sides at least, and the main shots, hopefully at our nice forty-five degree angle, must hit from these three or four sides. It's going to be tough when the actor comes to the edge of the stage, and the light hitting from the far side spills out into the first few rows. Curing this puts us through our paces: higher angles, lower readings, and sneaky from-the-side nibbles—all the tricks. We fight for every bit of light and every foot of acting area. The dull alternative is keeping actors away from the edge.

If you're lucky, the room will be intimate, and some low intensity light will do, or an actor framed by his halo (light from the other side) will be well enough seen for short moments. If you're lucky, the ceiling won't be so high and the lighting slots forced so far away by seating that all your beams are long. If you're lucky the ceiling won't be so low that you can't get any bite into the areas unless your units are all full flood.

Top light can still do its job as it did in the prosceniums, and that edge of light framing an actor is still needed to pull the figure out of the wall or away from the far-side audience. That is where magical things happen on an open stage—that glorious edge glow on the human figure with a surrounding crowd.

Color is difficult: if you hit with cool from one side and warm from another, one audience tier will spend the whole evening watching a blue face. Working with only pale tints can make the job look weak, but you can be saved by strong motivated light. Projections, shafts of light, cast glows—these help organize and enliven an open stage, and can be the only scenic organization when you're "out there". They create a lively strong side and excuse the weak side. Use them. Invent them.

Color toning from overhead fresnels or scoops is valuable,

because you're often looking at empty stage floor and it can't go dead.

Cuing is more fun because you truly compose your stage with light and you lead the attention of the audience with it. We saw some of this in the chapter on levels and cues. Again, remember that you can be leading whole heads to turn, not just eyes.

Generalizations are awful if you take them for advice, but great fun to stimulate thought. In this difficult chapter, we even run out of generalizations. More than ever, you have to study the particular stage and each particular moment, and knit this kind of lighting stitch by meticulous stitch. Give your designer time, and a lot of ideas.

16 *"Our Town"*

It may help to describe a simple production of a familiar play. *Our Town* was toured in Japan, Korea, and Singapore. We anticipated good equipment, but set-up time was to be a scanty four hours and translated instructions always cut into that time. We would use equipment available in the theatres: a new situation each time. The plot would have to be light and the cues as simple and as few as possible.

This was a production of the National Theatre of the Deaf, directed meticulously by Mack Scism. Visual language demands good visibility; you can't talk with your hands in the dark. The language form itself, new on stage to the Orient, was the stylistic focus of the production. Elaborate effects would take a back seat. Simplicity does not necessarily mean skimpy equipment. A bank of twenty beam projectors can create a nice sunrise over Grover's Corners, and that could be called one simple statement. In our case, however, simple did imply minimal.

In the above we're starting towards our concept, but don't expect it to emerge as a tight definition. Let's continue. As a piece of trellis is pushed on to the stage, the playwright says, "There's some scenery for those of you who think they have to have scenery." In his own introduction, Mr. Wilder says, "The scorn of verisimilitude throws all the greater emphasis on the ideas which the play hopes to offer."[1]

We seem headed towards suggesting our effects, and not engulfing the performance with them. Here's more background to the concept: Donald Malcolm's lovely and helpful praise of José Quintero's 1959 production. From *The New Yorker,* April 11:

Our Town is an oddly artless work of art that solves the special problems of the theatre by ignoring them. Its author, Thornton Wilder, is much like an acrobat who modestly declines to try anything as difficult as walking the tightwire and is content simply to dance along the same

[1]A. R. Fulton, *Drama and Theater,* New York: Henry Holt & Co., 1946.

"I heard a voice commanding a horse to be still, and saw Lysis reined in at the line, his left hand grasping the bridle, his right with the torch in it held straight up. The trumpet sounded, hoofs drummed on the earth; the torch-flame leaned backward on the air, and the sound of cheering followed it like smoke."

—Mary Renault

route on thin air . . . step by subtle step, the spectator is coaxed into constantly greater exertions of his imagination. When the milkman's horse becomes restive, the Stage Manager obliges with the necessary whicker. When an irascible old lady is called for, he pitches his voice an octave higher and delivers her line himself . . . By the middle of the first act, when the Stage Manager declares it to be evening, the spectator finds that it *is* evening, and such an evening as no expenditure for lights or scenery could possibly duplicate.

The bare stage, the few tables and chairs and the stepladders are all essential to this play. Would the bareness be understood in the Orient as we understand it here? Professionals are always wary that sparsity might be interpreted as penury, and on an international tour, supported by our State Department, this misunderstanding must be avoided. Also, we could not know if the stages would look like bare stages in the tradition for which Wilder wrote. A plaster sky, for example, demands treatment, and is not the symbol of non-scenery conveyed by the usual brick back wall.

We added two elements to emphasize the playwright's scorn of scenic illusion. The lighting instruments would all be in plain sight, both overhead and on the sides. Also, to occasionally remind us that we weren't being fooled in the usual way, the Stage Manager would signal for the light cues when he changed day to night, the homes to the drug store, and so forth. Just a snap of the fingers towards an offstage electrician. We could then drift imperceptibly from these sudden light cues into the inner variations: the ladder might dim down slightly when George is called to the kitchen, and the kitchen light could come up gently at that moment.

The following descriptions of the instruments used, and how some cues were set up, may be too detailed to hold your interest. Just skim it. You can always come back to it another time.

The simple light plot established ten areas. Downstage of the two homes the stage was divided into stage right, stage center and stage left. The Stage Manager strolls here, or pauses for a longer chat in one of these areas. The stringbean scene could play in the brightened stage left area and Emily's pre-wedding breakdown stage right. Each area would need at least four spots

"Screwed at its axis against the side, a swinging lamp slightly oscillates in Jonah's room; and the ship, heeling over towards the wharf with the weight of the last bail received, the lamp, flame and all, though in slight motion, still maintains a permanent obliquity with reference to the room; though, in truth, infallibly straight itself, it but made obvious the false, lying levels among which it hung. The lamp alarms and frightens Jonah; as lying in his berth his tormented eyes roll round the place, and this thus far successful fugitive finds no refuge for his restless glance. But that contradiction in the lamp more and more appals him. The floor, the ceiling, and the side, are all awry. 'Oh! so my conscience hangs in me!' he groans, 'straight upward, so it burns; but the chambers of my soul are all in crookedness!' "

—Herman Melville

from the front of the house: two from left and two from right, each instrument angling in at about 45°.

Upstage of these three apron areas we planned Doc Gibb's kitchen stage right (we called it area four) and Editor Webb's kitchen stage left (area five). These areas were a touch too far upstage for front of house spots, and slightly too far downstage for comfortable first pipe angles. We had to use both positions. Big fresnels hit from the first pipe and spotlights hit from the front of house, attempting, again, to come in from 45°. Thus the stage right kitchen was hit from the first pipe by one or two spots from the stage right end of the pipe, and one or two from just past the center of the pipe. The stage left kitchen reversed this. These angles created good modeling for the faces and gave us tight areas that didn't wander, clearly defining the rooms. Because the fresnel angles were steep and from the sides, we needed fill for the faces. The best solution for these would be to hit from the front, one or two spots from each side for each area.

If you've counted, you've noted that we used four or eight spots per area. In Tokyo we played a huge house with the first pipe high to ease balcony sight lines. We needed powerful narrow-beam instruments and we even doubled up. In Seoul, the theatre and stage was tiny, the first pipe low, the instruments powerful with wide angles, and one unit per position was enough.

Ideally, we should have had a third set of instruments for the night scenes, in different colors. Instead, we used one special to warm each area from the first pipe. A cool wash of four spotlights from the front of the house supplied the customary blue "surround" of night.

So far, counting instruments, we have at most thirty-four, used in five areas, one wash, and two specials.

We established another area between the two houses. This was useful when the women walked downstage after choir practice, to fill out the stage in the big wedding scene, and was the key light for the youngsters at their strawberry sodas. Though farther upstage than the downstage areas, it was an easy shot from the front of the house because it was center and comfortable angles could be found. We called this area six.

"A nail nailing its shadow to a high board . . ."

—Eudora Welty

The stepladders were upstage of the kitchens, and were called areas seven and eight. Each ladder was hit by a single spotlight from the first pipe. When Emily climbs her stage left ladder and faces George, a unit from stage right caught her full in the face. George had the reverse. A second unit in medium blue from the second pipe was focused straight down on him or her for a halo of evening color. Here we committed—and got away with—a cardinal sin. We put dissimilar lights into the same area control. Ideally, the blue downlight might stay on at nearly full when the face light dimmed. Usually an effect light and an acting light do different things and shouldn't be linked. But it worked in this case because the actors helped us. When the youngsters weren't featured, they took a step down the ladder or turned away slightly. Also penurious, and also a sin, we opened George's face beam slightly to hit sister Rebecca when she crowded into his window.

The choir was center, upstage of the ladders. Again, we called this an area, though it had only two lamps and both might have been specials for more sensitive control. The choirmaster, Simon Stimson, faced stage right and was hit from the right end of the second pipe, which was about twelve feet upstage of the first pipe. Another spot hit the choir from the left end of that pipe. Stimson's spot was clear and sharply focused, the choir's was tinted lavender and flooded. The relationship of color and intensity held when bright or dim (up and down on dimmer).

There was a tenth area. A lamp from each end of the second pipe hit the preacher and family upstage at the wedding.

Adding twelve lamps to the count, we now had forty-six. We now added side light: two booms per side. These swept the entire stage, which is the virtue of low and level-shooting units: they catch all in their light, both near or far. We could also reach these instruments easily in intermission for a color change. These units intruded the most, pictorially, and we placed them carefully to compose the stage. On big stages we used four lamps per boom, on smaller stages two were enough. Add sixteen lamps.

Another major statement was blue downlights. We used fresnels or even scoops when fresnels were not available. We placed four on the first pipe, four on the second, and four on the

"For love is the enemy of haste; it takes count of passing days, of men who pass away, of a fine art matured slowly in the course of years and doomed in a short time to pass away, too, and be no more. Love and regret go hand in hand in this world of changes swifter than the shifting of the clouds reflected in the mirror of the sea."

—Joseph Conrad

third. All in sight, these helped our blatant stagecraft. Besides the light on the actors, the instruments themselves gave us a handsome blue celestial oval above. A touch romantic, perhaps, but the constant cool wash filled and soothed the ugliness of some of the unmasked stages. Thornton Wilder's aim may have been a bare stage, but we never thought that he meant an ugly stage. We controlled these fresnels pipe by pipe. Add twelve units: we now have seventy-four.

Now for more specials. Downstage right, out on the apron, one stand held a single spot—our sunrise. When the stage manager told us that another day had begun, this unit came on at his gesture, and we had a morning beam for Doc Gibbs and the paperboy. It was for those of us who think they have to have lighting effects: it was the equivalent of the trellises. It seemed to state our no-nonsense approach to lighting. In the second act, the Stage Manager himself removed the gel, and the spot sharpened the afternoon brightness on the stringbean scene and the street scene just before the sodas.

Other specials were a flooded fresnel on the second pipe, to give a lavender highlight to the black funeral umbrellas; and another for the graves from the first pipe. A pale blue fresnel helped Mr. and Mrs. Gibbs when they walked out into the moonlight to smell the heliotrope. Another was needed for Editor Webb a moment later when he talked to Emily at her stepladder. Another spot hit a far upstage position for Doc Gibbs when he first entered in Act I, and this was also used for Editor Webb upstage with the Constable. We needed three spots to pick out faces precisely in the graveyard, and, as this play was blocked, an ever-so-subtle follow spot could have helped here. Remember, however, that in most situations even a few dozen specials can be cheaper than paying for a follow spot operator.

Remembering the two kitchen warming specials, and adding the above nine, we now count eighty-three lamps ganged into twenty dimmers, plus eleven specials on individual control, one dimmer for each. Sparse indeed. We then found that the twelve blue downlights could all be in one dimmer, since they moved as one; but twelve-thousand-watt dimmers are rare, so we continued with three dimmers. We needed one more special lamp:

"It was the hour when the shapes in the kitchen darkened and voices bloomed."

—Carson McCullers

a pedestal light—the bare-bulb night light of the stage. We plugged this into a receptacle, saving dimmer control. It was a 100-watt-lamp, and snapped on and off.

In theatres where we had enough dimmer control, we could divide our boom shots and have right and left and downstage and upstage control. With less control, we chose right and left control, because the bare stage of *Our Town* gracefully received the upstage light when actors did not venture there, and it could therefore remain. That is an example of the choices that can be made. When we were short of dimmers, we could re-plug and re-color before the funeral scene. We shifted the boom gels to pale blues and lavenders and split off the upstage booms which, in that scene, did stain distractingly in the fragile twilight of the rainy funeral day. Re-plugging is poor practice and its possible consequences are described in the chapter on Manners.

Our color was simple. The front wash was a medium blue, not in the blue-green family, but drier, less theatrical: towards cobalt. The downlights were in the same tonality but deeper.

The rain lights for the umbrellas and the graves were in lavenders, not as pale as mere tints, nor as dark or lurid as night club tones. The only theatrically brilliant color was the sunrise spotlight which, as we used it, made a point of artificiality. In the area lights and the booms we used pale tints—rather ordinary acting light. For warms, we used both clear and the standard Bastard Amber (AKA Flame or Gold). For cools, we used pale Blues and Special Lavender. These conventional acting tones were not a challenge to the audience, and they worked well for ordinary good modelling and visibility.

There was no curtain. Our pre-set featured the pedestal night light and the blue downlights. The Stage Manager walked on, and cue one was a slow and almost imperceptible dim-up of the downstage areas as he checked the furniture. The houselights dimmed only enough to alert the audience. A stagehand came on and the Stage Manager handed him the pedestal light which he snapped off and carried out. There was enough light by now to bring the Stage Manager downstage, and it grew with him as he moved. He flicked his hand and the houselights snapped off. He began. His first speech described the town, and the night

"Returning, I had to cross before the looking-glass; my fascinated glance involuntarily explored the depth it revealed. All looked colder and darker in that visionary hollow than in reality: and the strange little figure there gazing at me, with a white face and arms specking the gloom, and glittering eyes of fear moving where all else was still, had the effect of a real spirit . . ."

—Charlotte Brontë

blues were now intense. He stood out in the slightly warm areas downstage. When he told us that another day had begun, he gestured for the sunrise spot, and the low-angled orange light was cast across stage. Then there was a follow cue that brought a glow to Mrs. Gibbs' kitchen as she entered. The Stage Manager continued his description and, as a separate cue, Mrs. Webb's kitchen area started up on her entrance. Doc Gibbs entered and moved downstage, and as he stepped into the sunrise the Stage Manager mentioned him again. The paper boy entered and chatted with the doctor. They were hit strongly from one side only, but they faced the light, diagonally downstage of them and the morning sharpness was emphasized by their unmodelled faces. Then Doc Gibbs skimmed the newspaper, and another cue subtly added downstage area light for his next conversation, with the milkman. When he finally entered his house, the kitchen light surged up as he crossed the threshold and his wife greeted him. The Webb kitchen brightened when Mrs. Webb called the children for breakfast, and then took its full brightness when they rushed on. The sunrise spot was now almost out: it had started dimming out when Doc Gibbs entered his home.

These were the first cues—the build-up to full light. After the children ate their hasty breakfasts, they hurried through imaginary doors as the downstage center area, now the street outside their homes, brightened. We didn't use the full width brightness downstage, but let them run out of the bright light to school as our attention went to the mothers, coming out into the sunlight for their morning chat. Their kitchens dimmed slightly. The downstage was bright, and bouncelight warmed the entire stage. Our opening blue tone had faded. We listened to the mothers until the Stage Manager dismissed them. After their exit, he moved into a side area downstage to vary the picture for his interviews with Professor Willard. That area rose slightly and the center area dimmed to help compose the stage.

These were the opening cues, the build: they were simple, logical, and unpretentious.

"Then, like a dense veil slowly falling from the starry sky on the two men, silence returned."

—Albert Camus

17 *Manners*

There is a lovely story, variously assigned, of a lighting designer who had completed focus and was running circuits. When the ninety-sixth and last circuit was seen, the producer spoke from the back of the dark auditorium. "I hated sixty-seven."

Tyrone Guthrie once put his hand on my shoulder at a similar moment and said that he doubted we'd want those four circuits of blues, our original image needn't be compromised, he'd been watching and now saw very clearly where we should go. "Regel now and save time," he advised. Sir Tyrone was usually right. In the same production I had asked for a luminous ceiling that might glow at the moment of God's sensed but unseen entrance into the small synagogue. The management and even the director had their doubts and it was costly. In my bones I knew it would work, and they gave me the chance to try. When all the circuits came on in technical rehearsal, Tony turned to me and whispered, 'Congratulations!' He whispered it at perfect volume, softly enough so that it was not trumpeted as self-serving generosity, but loudly enough so that the producer could hear.

A thoughtful boost makes it easy to work through the night. It shouldn't matter, because professionals do their best always. But some directors make this painful. Once we put on a complex one-setter in a long day in New Haven. It looked right, and we were tired but satisfied. The director came to the theatre at midnight. He could now have extra hours of onstage rehearsal. We glanced over, expecting a pleasant word. His knuckles were white on the arms of his seat, his face ghastly. Was he crying? "What's wrong?" was the obvious question. "Woody would never have a desk chair that ugly," he said. We changed the chair in twenty seconds the next morning. Some jobs are lonely.

A producer called soon after I had started work on his play. Could we make a Monday night in Boston? Hard—the show was big, heavy in all departments, and fussy. "It'll look rotten," I said. "Will it look better in the dump? We gotta, Pappy," was

"Frost on the grass like condensed moonlight."

—Joyce Cary

his characteristic reply. "We can't miss out on Theatre Guild subscription for the whole run in that town." We ran two shows on Saturday in New Haven, were loaded into six forty-foot trucks by seven on Sunday morning, and got the curtain up by eight on Monday night. We never left the theatre for a meal. In the middle of the first act, the producer pointed out that the damn stage was so damn dark during that damn scene that the only damn light on the damn stage was reflected from the damn spectacles of the damn first row customers. I lost my not-famous cool, and answered loudly that six weeks ago he'd been only a businessman, and suddenly now he was a great flapping artist. We walked around the block. Half way, we both started to laugh.

More wonderful was the opening night in New York when a pool of light simply failed to come on. I knew why instantly, and so did my assistant; we'd forgotten a re-plug after the photo call. He was off in a flash, but wasn't the first to reach the boards, where the electrician was already working to correct the error. The playwright was there first. "That man is fired!" he screamed helpfully. Sir Tyrone, again the director, had also run backstage. The producer brought up the rear. Everyone seemed distressed not to see Frederick March deliver his major speech. "Happily," said Sir Tyrone later, "I didn't arrive in time to do any real damage."

I met the playwright moments later, crossing Forty-fifth Street. He lifted me by my tuxedo lapels. "You've ruined my play!" he said. I looked down. "All of it?" I asked foolishly. "Forty percent," he conceded, and set me down. "Two years of my life." "At forty percent that's about ten months," I said. "How can this happen," he mused, "that other people come in and ruin your work? Theatre is so cruel." "Write novels," I said meanly, and he bought me a drink.

Extending this, I fell into conversation, at a gathering, with a famous novelist. He said that he'd written a play. I murmured my sympathy. I reminded him of Bill Gibson's thought in *The Seesaw Log* that writing a play and then losing control to the swarm of experts who put it on stage was like doing a painting with colored mice.

His answer was interesting. Yes, because he was established,

"The shadow of the masts and rigging, with the never-furled riding-sail, rolled to and fro on the heaving deck on the moonlight; and the pile of fish by the stern shone like a dump of fluid silver."

—Rudyard Kipling

he had good control over his novels, and a publisher wouldn't even deny him authority over typeface, paper stock, cover design, and so forth. But he couldn't control how it was read. A page at a time in the w.c.? Drowsy-time at night? Attentively in one excited gulp? As for his play, to be sure it might not have the actors or action he envisioned when he wrote it. He would fight those battles and lose some. "But when the curtain goes up," he said, "it will be to a roomful of people who are there for the same purpose and they'll all be seeing the same thing through the same span of time."

When we started this book, we saw it from the abused director's point of view. We saw protective and uncommunicative artists and technicians. It works both ways. The point is, how do we get the best work? The answer is that we don't lose our sense of humor, and there are no other rules. But there is a list of suggestions.

Be "up front". Spend time and thought. What do you want? What are the key scenes? Can you form images for them? What are the key entrances? How do you want this actress to appear at this moment? What are the moments that might be underlined by light—and what kind of light?

Speak out clearly, but also listen. Your designer has spent hours looking at the script from his or her point of view. Is it understood? Attention has been paid to details that you've not yet faced. Is that the way you want it? Visualize it now, in sharp focus if possible, because technical matters get frozen on paper and may be hard to adjust, harder than moving an actor, which can often be done in an instant and on whim. Make your convictions clear but never be afraid of stating your uncertainties.

A designer must not resist the difficulties, the questions, the moves that are not yet clear. Ideas that arrive late must be welcomed if they improve the work. Technical annoyance is childish. Difficult alterations are not an interruption to a designer's work, but part of its nature—and the ultimate test of skill.

Your designers should watch as many rehearsals as possible, and you'll save grief later if you welcome them, sit a moment, and be sure that you all see the same thing. Listen carefully for thoughts you've missed: specialists have insights you need.

"At the end of June, and with the start of a new moon, Ramadan begins. For the Arabs, Ramadan is a month of abstinence. As dark comes on, a colored string is stretched in the air, and when the string grows invisible, conch horns signal the Arabs to the food and drink that during the day they cannot touch."

—Truman Capote

If you've not been there, it's hard to understand how under-valued a designer can feel. Few critics talk about their work in an informed way. Few producers resist the line, "it won't sell one more ticket". But the matrix of the play is what your design-ers do. The visual quality of the actors' "surround" is encom-passing and inseparable and often generative of the riches of the play.

Keep asking questions. It's the best way to build good work. What does this or that mean on the plot? Will beams of light crash into the chandelier? Are there positions on stage that are really tough to light? You will not be a pest if you ask questions to get information. Never ask questions to show how smart you are.

When does your designer want you around? Try to be there, and be there on time—but don't fret when technical things don't start on the dot. Get coffee.

Don't harass your designer. Once upon a time I was designing a set for a well-known director. He would arrive late, toss off his cape, and then we'd sit at a drawing table he'd set up for me in his "studio". "Where will you put that door?" "Oh, about up here." "No no, I mean exactly." "About a foot in." "But what about the servant's door, that's next to it?" "Sure, it'll be there." "Well, let's be clear on the point. If you put the big door eleven inches in, and it's a thirty-inch door, let's see, here on the scale rule . . . if we give it a five-and-half-inch frame, that adds eleven inches, give a half—no—three-quarters of an inch clearance, that's forty-one and three-quarters plus the eleven, then a six-inch space, no seven, then the twenty-two-inch frameless ser-vant's door—gets a bit tight. David, you'd better start the big door in ten and one-half inches."

What an unhappy job! How I longed to be home at my own board. Weeks later, after the set was built, the director changed his mind and wanted the doors *reversed,* which was the real question from the start. It would cost a few thousand dollars, and I refused, backed cheerfully by the exhausted producer. There was a wretched showdown in the rehearsal room.

Later that day I met a more friendly director on Eighth Avenue. He leaned over and whispered to me, "I just heard through the grapevine that you and _____ had a terrible

"The soft night was all about them. Curtains of shadow hung amid the leaves."

—Gustave Flaubert

row and he cried behind the piano." "I don't know," I said, "that must have been after I left." He leaned closer. "I didn't know it was a musical," he said.

Don't lose your sense of humor. But what does that mean? It doesn't mean "Ha ha". There's a great deal of laughter in theatre, the sad laughter of mistakes and failures. But the laughter Fred Coe and I shared in Boston was with the knowledge that we'd both done our best, that we'd work the next day to make the scene perfect, and that we wouldn't lose this one. Then you can laugh, and that's the visible tip of the sense of humor I'm talking about.

There's a moment that comes to many productions and it's called "Survival Time". It's the moment when the work is obviously going down the drain, and many will jump to escape the suction. For some, the moment comes before the job really begins: it's in their nature. Every show is only their showcase. Others work with all good will, but foresee doomsday and pull out of discussion. Some survive by doing their job well. When a famous comic decided that he should ad lib and clown because the audience was coming to see him and not Richard Rodgers' musical (which the comic himself had spoiled, and that's why it was Survival Time), only one performer didn't put up with it. She did her job as rehearsed. She got credit for that: an unusual way of surviving.

"Survival Time" could be a book in itself. How can it be avoided? Is it only the subtle aura of half-promised jobs to come that constrains us to good behavior? Some don't care about that, some count on the forgetfulness of our profession, some know that a job unadjusted to the changed needs of the production will be more visible as a separate tour de force, standing out and praised. There's no answer. Some teams work well, win or lose. Treasure them.

Here's a team that worked, and a shining example of "Manners". At eight one night, before the eight-thirty première of a major full-length ballet, George Balanchine remembered something. "I know how we must end it," he said, and gave a brief description. The stage manager ran for his cache of slender airplane cable, the flyman brought in a free pipe downstage, the carpenter found his tiny wire clamps, the prop man dug out his

"I stepped on deck; the sky, still wholly dark, was truly the iron sky of Homer's poems, indifferent to man's woes and joys alike."

—Marguerite Yourcenar

black paint, and I ran across the street to a restaurant for some vinegar. We made a loop of the wire, Arthur Mitchell came on stage and Mr. B. showed him how to step on to the loop and wrap his arms in the wire with a flourish. The flyman took him up, and he would be gently soaring into the forest branches as the final curtain fell. We tried it again, set our marks, and wrote in the cue with the follow spot operator. We painted the cable black. It was only eight-twenty.

No one said, "Gee, why the creeps can't he make up his mind", or "Are you kidding, it's eight o'clock", or worse . . . We just did it. Why bother not to? We were working and thinking along with Mr. Balanchine and with Ronnie Bates, a champion man and stage manager who never played the divisive game of "them and us". If only it could have been that way forever.

The vinegar? That's a mild acid. It dries and etches the oily wire before the paint grips it. I was nervous, and it gave me something to do.

"It was very dark and empty in the passage. Not a soul, as though everything had been carried out. Very quietly, on tiptoe, he went into the sitting-room: the whole room was flooded with moonlight. Everything there was as before: the chairs, the looking-glass, the yellow sofa, and the pictures in the frames. A huge, round, copper-red moon was staring through the windows. 'It's the moon that makes everything so still,' thought Raskolnikov. 'It must be asking a riddle.' He stood and waited. He waited a long time, and the more silent the moon was, the more violently did his heart beat, so that he was even beginning to feel a pain. And still not a sound."

—Fyodor Dostoyevsky

Glossary

ADAPTER. A device that helps the wrong plug fit into the right socket and vice versa.

ADDITIVE PROCESS. Colored light from two or more sources hits a surface and mixes (reflects together) creating another color.

ALTERNATING CURRENT, AC. Ordinary household current, sixty complete cycles every second—it reverses direction one hundred and twenty times per second.

ALZAK. A trade name for finishing a reflector surface to make it durable and heat resistant.

AMBIENT LIGHT. Usually, the light onstage competing when you're trying to punch through with a projection or special effect.

AMPERE. Named after André Ampère, French physicist, 1775–1836. An arbitrary unit to measure the rate of flow, or intensity, of electric current.

ANGLES OF INCIDENCE AND REFLECTION. The first is the angle at which a beam of light hits a surface; the second the angle at which it bounces off. These angles are equal.

ANODE. The positive terminal. Current enters here. The cathode is the negative. Carbon arcs use these terminals.

ARC. A lighting instrument, Arc or Arclight, usually a follow spot and powerful. Also, to be more precise, the arc itself, which is the steady leap of a brilliant spark from one electrified carbon rod to another.

AREA. An Area, often *Acting Area,* usually means one part of the stage that you light and control as an entity.

ARM. *See* SIDEARM.

AUTOTRANSFORMER. A kind of dimmer. See Chapter 7.

BABY, BABY SPOT. Lighting instruments pass puberty at 500 watts. Those less powerful, often damn useful because of their small size, can be called Babies.

BACK LIGHT. Usually light directed down on or from slightly

Every minute that white wooly plain which covered one-half of the moor was drifting closer and closer to the house. Already the first thin wisps of it were curling across the golden square of the lighted window. The farther wall of the orchard was already invisible, and the trees were standing out of a swirl of white vapour. As we watched it the fog-wreaths came crawling around both corners of the house and rolled slowly into one dense bank, on which the upper floor and the roof floated like a strange ship upon a shadowy sea . . . as the fog-bank flowed onward we fell back before it until we were half a mile from the house, and still that dense white sea, with the moon silvering its upper edge, swept slowly and inexorably on. . . .

. . . Lestrade gave a yell of terror and threw himself face downward upon the ground. I sprang to my feet, my inert hand grasping my pistol, my mind paralyzed by the dreadful shape which had sprung out upon us from the shadows of the fog. A hound it was, an enormous coal-black hound, but not such a hound as mortal eyes have ever seen. Fire burst from its open mouth, its eyes glowed with a smouldering glare, its muzzle and hackles and dewlap were outlined in flickering flame. Never in the delerious dream of a disordered brain could anything more savage, more appalling, more hellish be conceived than that dark form and savage face which broke upon us out of the wall of fog.

—Sir Arthur Conan Doyle

behind an actor. It might also mean light illuminating translucent scenery from behind.

BACKING LIGHT. Light for backings, such as door backings (hall-
ways) or small skies outside windows.

BACKING STRIP. Perhaps a small striplight to achieve the above.

BAFFLE. A preventor, or the prevention, of unwanted light
escape.

BALCONY, BALCONY RAIL. Position for instruments on front of
balcony.

BALLAST. A resistance unit added to the flow of current to an
arc: it limits or stabilizes the flow. Sometimes used to denote the Ghost Load needed to balance a resistance dimmer.

BANK, DIMMER BANK. A group of dimmers, a section of a dimmer board. One might 'add another bank' of dimmers, of
pre-sets, etc.

BARN DOORS. A set of flippers, like horse blinders, that can be
mounted on a spotlight, usually a Fresnel, to cut off a part
of the beam or cut down unwanted spill.

BASE. A *Lamp Base* is the part of a lamp that connects it to the
instrument and the current. A *Boom Base* is the bottom of
the boom.

BASTARD AMBER. A useful color for lighting actors, amber and
slightly rosy.

BAYONET BASE. A type of lamp base that inserts and twists to
hold or lock.

BEAM. The light from an instrument. Also a position for mounting instruments in the ceiling of the auditorium.

BEAM PROJECTOR. A lensless instrument producing an intense
and narrow beam.

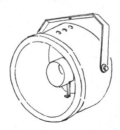

Beam Projector

"Is it against the law for a man to be down on all fours beside a road, barking in a perfectly civil manner?" demanded the lady.

"No, ma'am," said the cop. He made no move to get on his motorcycle, however, and go on about his business. There was just the quiet chugging of the cycle engine and the auto engine, for a time.

"I'll tell you how it was, Officer," said the man, in a crisp new tone. "We were settling a bet. O.K.?"

"O.K.," said the cop. "Who win?" There was another pulsing silence.

"The lady bet," said her husband, with dignity, as though he were explaining some important phase of industry to a newly hired clerk, "the lady bet that my eyes would shine like a cat's do at night, if she came upon me suddenly close to the ground alongside the road. We had passed a cat, whose eyes gleamed. We had passed several persons, whose eyes did *not* gleam—"

"Simply because they were above the light and not under it," said the lady. "A man's eyes would gleam like a cat's if people were ordinarily caught by headlights at the same angle as cats are." The cop walked over to where he had left his motorcycle, picked it up, kicked the standard out, and wheeled it back.

"A cat's eyes," he said, "are different than yours and mine. Dogs, cats, skunks, it's all the same. They can see in a dark room."

"Not in a *totally* dark room," said the lady.

"Yes, they can," said the cop.

"No, they can't; not if there is no light at all in the room, not if it's absolutely *black,*" said the lady.

—James Thurber

BIPOST. A kind of lamp base: two prongs that stick into two holes. Often used for big lamps.

BIRDSEYE. A small lamp with a built-in silvered reflector. You see this style of lamp in outdoor lighting or in art galleries. Similar to a PAR.

BISCUIT. A small loudspeaker, often hung near the boards. The stage manager's voice carries through it, announcing cues,

BLACK LIGHT. *See* ULTRAVIOLET.

BLACKOUT. Rarely complete or well done.

BLOOM. A blaze of light from a lamp or a reflection. You've seen this happen in old films. We usually avoid it, but it can be lovely.

BOOM. An upright pipe for mounting lighting instruments.

BOOMERANG. The long way to say Boom. Also can mean a manual or remotely controlled color changer in front of a spotlight.

BORDERLIGHT, BORDER. Usually a horizontal striplight, hung above a stage. Also a cloth border—overhead masking—as in wing and border.

BOUNCE, BOUNCELIGHT. Where the light goes after it hits the floor.

BOX. Electrical wires come into this, where they can be spliced or hooked into a receptacle.

BOX BOOMS. Booms mounted in the auditorium boxes or on the side walls of the auditorium.

BREAKER. *See* CIRCUIT BREAKER.

BRIDGE. An overhead walkway, hopefully narrow and in the right place. Lamps can be hung from it and you can creep along it to focus them. You might operate a follow spot from it.

BRUSH. A sliding contactor, as in an electric motor or a dimmer.

BULB. The glass envelope for the filament. Bulb, filament, and base make up a lamp.

BUMP-UP. A sudden dim-up.

BUNCH LIGHT. An old pan-like reflector with many lamps screwed to it to give a big flood of light. Films use a similar device—many reflector lamps bunched together. Often each has its off-on switch. Thus, a 'nine-light' has nine dimming possibilities.

"The darkness was racing toward them now and the light expiring. Narouz suddenly cried, "Now is the moment. Look there." He clapped his hands loudly and shouted across the water, startling his companion who followed his pointed finger with raised head. "What?" the dull report of a gun from the furtherest boat shook the air and suddenly the sky line was sliced in half by a new flight, rising more slowly and dividing earth from air in a pink travelling wound; like the heart of a pomegranate staring through its skin. Then, turning from pink to scarlet, flushed back into white and fell to the lake level like a shower of snow to melt as it touched the water—"Flamingo," they both cried and laughed, and the darkness snapped upon them, extinguishing the visible world.

—Lawrence Durrell

CABLE. Our name for sturdy flexible electric wire, with a round heavy rubber insulating cover. We usually use 12 gauge cable. As the numbers go down, it gets fatter. #16 is the household zip cord gauge.

CALIBRATE. To adjust the dimmer controls to make the lamps dim smoothly and evenly. Also, a dimmer should read consistently with the other dimmers on the same board.

CANDELABRA BASE. A screw-in base, smaller than an ordinary household base.

CANDLE POWER. A measure of light intensity. *See* FOOT CANDLE.

CAPACITY. The electrical load that a dimmer, a cable, or a fuse can handle.

CATHODE. *See* ANODE.

CHAINS. Safety chains can prevent lighting instruments or other things hung overhead from falling and entering your body.

CHANNEL. A fancy dimmer board term, meaning, essentially, a dimmer.

CHESEBORO. A trade name. A type of clamp, fastening two pipes together. Sidearms can fasten to booms using these.

CINEMOID. A trade name for a brand of plastic color filters.

CIRCUIT. A complete path of electricity to supply a lamp, a dimmer, etc.

CIRCUIT BREAKER. If overheated, this switch will shut off: a fuse function. When the overload has been corrected and it cools, you can switch it on again.

CLAMP, C-CLAMP. Lighting units have clamps that attach them to a pipe. A sidearm will have one to attach it to a boom, etc.

CODE. The laws or rules concerning safe electrical practice. Mostly the *don'ts:* don't use circuits without fuses, don't run cables across the aisles.

COLOR. Light waves in the visible spectrum (rainbow) plus white if you wish. Also we use the word to denote the gel or plastic or glass color filter. We also say, "Let's color those lamps."

COLOR FRAME. A thin metal frame holding the gel or plastic

The damp night air was fragrant all about him, the gloom of trees surrounded him, the small sweet stars shone high above, and behind him the lights of the city floated like fireworks in the darkness.

—Robert Nathan

glass color filter. This frame is made to slip into grooves which hold it in front of the lamp or lens.

COLOR MEDIA, COLOR FILTERS. What you use to color the instrument: gel, glass, plastics.

COLOR TEMPERATURE. There is a scale describing just how white-hot a white-hot filament is.

COLOR WHEEL. A wheel that turns in front of an instrument. You can insert the colors of your choice into its pie-slice divisions, and then quickly swing to the one you want. Sometimes these are rotated by a motor to vary color, as in a night club or a firelight effect.

COMPANY SWITCH. The big outlet in a theatre where you tap in to supply electricity to your portable boards.

COMPLEMENTARY COLORS. Two colors that mix (on a surface) to make white. Rarely perfect.

COMPUTER BOARD. A dimmer board using computer hardware to remember, activate, and display circuits.

CONDENSING SYSTEM. Two or more lenses carefully spaced in one lighting instrument to gather the light coming from the source or reflector and narrow it into an intense beam.

CONDUIT. Permanently-placed protective tubing in which insulated wires run.

CONNECTOR. Usually one of the many kinds of plugs, male or female, connecting one cable to another.

CONSOLE. The control part of a modern dimmer board. You sit at this and fiddle with the lights.

CONTACTOR. A metal piece that makes the actual contact to allow electrical flow. Often it is remotely controlled.

CONTROL BOARD. Another name for switchboard or dimmer board.

CONVENIENCE OUTLET. The common home-style wall outlet.

CONVEX LENS. A lens with one curved-out surface and the other surface flat, is called a plano-convex lens. Sometimes both sides are convex, like the side view of a football.

COOKIE. A name for a metal cut-out plate used for pattern projection.

COOL COLORS. Blues and greens. Lavenders and purples, usually cools, might be used as warms.

CORD. A cable, but usually suggesting a lighter gauge, quite flexible.

COUNT. As in, say, a ten-count cue, meaning that you do the cue in ten counts. Usually the counts are one second each, but one can have one's individual style.

COVE. A slot for lighting instruments in the ceiling or side walls of an auditorium.

CRESCENT, CRESCENT WRENCH. A trade name for the adjustable end wrench used to tighten and loosen C-clamps, yokes, etc.

CROSS-FADE. Going from one cue to another by dimming down what must be dimmed down and dimming up what must be dimmed up—at the same time.

CROSSOVER PIPE. A pipe used to carry cable overhead to the other side of the stage, to supply booms, etc. on that side.

CUCALORIS, CUKE, COOKIE. A cut-out metal piece that can be inserted in some instruments, usually ellipsoidal spots, to project a pattern. Called a pattern also.

CUE. The planned and timed operation of changing light levels. See Chapter 9.

CUE SHEET. Simply the notation of cues.

CURRENT FLOW. Measured in Amperes, this is the movement of electricity—of electrons through a conductor.

CUT-OFF. A device such as barn doors or a top hat to control the beam of light—usually after it has come out of the lens—but the framing shutters of an Ellipsoidal Reflector spot could be called cut-offs.

CYCLORAMA, CYC. The sky cloth, though it might mean a plaster sky.

DEAD. Not carrying current at the moment. Having died, such as a burned-out lamp. Also, insulated, as in a dead-front board, which gives protection to the operator.

DEAD SPOT. Where your actor goes into relative darkness and it's someone's fault.

DIFFUSE. As in reflection or spread. Think of light through frosted glass.

DIM. Not bright. Or the verb: to change the intensity of a lamp. You can dim it down or (we say) dim it up.

DIMMER. See Chapter 7. A device to dim a lamp.

DIMMER CURVE. The relationship between the setting of the dimmer and the intensity of the lamp. Unlike a bad gas gauge, three-quarters should mean just that, one-tenth just that, etc.

DIP. A bad spot in a dimming curve, or when your cross-fade doesn't go smoothly, or when your local power plant is hit by lightning and wavers. *Also see* LAMP DIP.

DIRECT CURRENT, DC. Current flows in one direction only. Often the only kind of current in old theatre installations.

DOUBLE-THROW SWITCH. Throw it one way, it turns on certain circuits. Throw it the other way, it turns on other circuits. "Off" is often in the middle.

DOWN LIGHT. An instrument or a wash from instruments that is focused nearly straight down.

DOWSER, DOUSER. A device such as a flap or sliding shutter to cut off the light from an instrument, usually an arc follow spot.

DROP BOX. An outlet box on a long cable that can be lowered from the grid to supply pipes, ladders, etc.

DUTCHMAN. A gimmick often containing an extra lens plus a slide or film holder. It then can be mounted in front of a spotlight to make it into a slide or effect projector.

EFFECT MACHINE. Usually a projector that produces moving projections (clouds, fire, waterfalls, etc.).

ELECTRICIAN. A member of the electrical crew (as opposed to property men, carpenters). Often we say "in electrics". Often a more exact title is possible: "Master Electrician" or "Front Man" (follow spot person).

ELECTRODE. An electrical pole or terminal.

ELECTRONIC. Too inexactly used in our work to be seriously defined, and too confusing to be humorously defined.

ELLIPSOIDAL REFLECTOR. A reflector made in the shape of part of an ellipsoid. The light source is placed within this shape at its axis—as if held within half an eggshell.

ELLIPSOIDAL SPOTLIGHT (Ellipsoidal Reflector Spotlight, ERS). The spotlight using this kind of reflector—see Chapter 2.

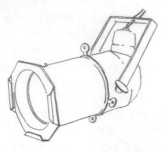

Ellipsoidal Spotlight

ENVELOPE. The glass part of a lamp—the bulb (as opposed to filament or base).

ERS. See ELLIPSOIDAL SPOTLIGHT, above.

FADE. Not necessarily fade out or dim down—can mean fade up or cross-fade. "Fade in" usually means to come up from dark.

FADER. The master handle that controls several dimmers or pre-sets.

FEED CABLE, FEEDER. The big cable that connects the switchboard to the juice. Sometimes the cables that serve multi-lamp units such as striplights.

FEMALE CONNECTORS. A traditional designation that can't be helped. The female plugs have the holes or grooves, the male plugs the stick-out parts or prongs.

FILAMENT. The part of a lamp, usually wire held in the glass envelope, that gets white-hot when electrified.

FILAMENT IMAGE. Instead of having a nice clear field of light, the reflector plays a trick on you and projects the image of the filament. You have to fool with the focus and the filament-reflector relationship to smooth this away.

FILL LIGHT. Usually washes from front, sides, or above that may not be critical acting light but are needed to give a sense of all-over general illumination or to smooth out the field of light.

FILTER. Usually the color media (gel, frost, etc.) placed in front of the lighting instrument.

FIRST PIPE, FIRST ELECTRIC. The first pipe upstage of the proscenium which, in our case, is used for mounting electrical units.

FLASH POT. Perhaps a metal box with an exposed wire or fuse in it which will ignite a powder when this fuse or wire becomes hot. This gives us a flash, smoke, a small explosion, etc.

FLIPPER. *See* BARN DOOR, CUT-OFF, etc.

FLOOD. To focus to a wide beam, as opposed to spot, meaning to focus to a narrow beam.

FLOODLIGHT. Usually lensless units to create a big glob of light. Can be one unit on a stand or a pipe or even a striplight used to wash the sky.

FLOOR POCKET. A receptacle for a plug, usually recessed into the stage floor and with a lid so you don't fall into it.

FLORESCENCE. Glows because it's become charged by light waves such as ultraviolet.

FOCAL LENGTH, FOCAL POINT. Focal point is where the rays of light that pass through the lens converge. The focal length is the distance between the centre of the lens and this point.

FOCUS. Aim and adjust the instrument and its light beam, used as a verb or noun. Also rather loosely, the correct relationship of a filament to reflector, lens, etc.

FOLLOW CUE. A cue that starts as soon as the cue before it is completed. The stage manager doesn't need to call it separately.

FOLLOW SPOT. Any unit used to "follow" a performer or group, operated by a person. There are some rare instances of automatic or remotely controlled units.

FOOT CANDLE. The measure of light intensity—light's version of horsepower or BTU. Theoretically the light cast by one candle on a surface of one square foot, one foot away.

FOOTLIGHTS, FOOTS. Lights in the stage floor downstage, usually on the apron, sometimes recessed, either strips or individual units. The British form is "Floats", probably from the days when wicks floated in oil.

FRESNEL (pronounced "fre-*nel*"). A type of lens, or a spotlight using that lens. See Chapter 2.

FROST. A color medium etched like frosted glass to soft-edge or spread a beam of light.

Fresnel

FUNNEL. A device to limit stray light or shape a beam. It's placed in front of the unit: it mounts in the color frame holder grooves.

FUSE. A device that melts or snaps off like a switch if there is an overload and the circuit (cable, dimmer, connecting wires) gets dangerously overloaded. Fuses can be the familiar screw-in plug fuses, or cartridge snap-in fuses.

GANG. To team up two or more instruments on the same circuit or two or more circuits into the same dimmer.

GEL FRAME. *See* COLOR FRAME.

GELATIN. Thin sheet color medium. Dyed animal gelatin. "Gel" is the classic stuff, replaced now to a large extent by plastics which fade more slowly, don't vanish quite as fast under high heat, and don't melt in the rain. To many, gel still has the prettiest colors.

GENERAL LIGHTING. Fill and washes from strips or scoops or spots: not specifically directed acting light. Can also mean area lighting as opposed to specials.

GHOST LOAD. Resistance, such as extra concealed instruments, added to a circuit which is to be dimmed by a resistance dimmer. These dimmers need to be filled close to their capacity to work correctly.

GOBO. A cut-out held in front of a lens to make a pattern of the light.

GRAND MASTER. A dimmer that is even bigger than the sub master or group masters. Take down this handle and a lot comes down with it.

GROUND. Literally, to take a wire to the ground or to some huge hunk of metal or the building. This could be the third wire in a cable (you've seen three-prong plugs and receptacles for heavier power tools, etc.). If there's a short circuit, the current has an easy alternative path rather than all going through you.

GROUND ROW. A floor striplight to light upwards on to a sky or scenic piece. It is sometimes hidden behind a low piece of scenery called by the same name.

HALF PLUG. A narrow stage plug: two can be inserted into one pocket. Also called SPLIT PLUG.

HALOGEN. Referring to a variety of gases used in lamps.

HANG. To place your instruments on stage where you want them for the show. This implies hanging from a pipe— clamping on. Not necessarily: you also "hang" your set, although scenery, like lights, may stand up on its own.

HEAD SPOT. A narrow beam for the face from a spotlight.

HIGH HAT. See FUNNEL—looks like a top hat open on top—hat rim fits in gel frame of instrument. Cuts off stray light.

HORIZON STRIP, HORIZONS. See GROUND ROW.

HOT. Current is on. Also can mean the high voltage wires carrying current as opposed to the neutral wire.

HOT POCKET. Non-dimming receptacle. May not even have a switch. See INDEPENDENT.

HOT SPOT. In the centre of the field of light cast by an instrument there may be the brightest part. Also, the opposite of dead spot.

HOUSE. The auditorium. House lights.

HOUSE BOARD. Probably the board operating the houselights, and some work lights. Not the show board.

HOUSE LIGHTS. The auditorium lights. Their careful use can be an important effect in the play.

HOUSING. The enclosing body of the lighting instrument.

HUE. The basic color: it can be dark or light, saturated or pale, full or greyed down.

IMAGE. The picture you project from a projection instrument.

INCANDESCENT. Glowing because it is hot: the incandescent lamp has a filament which does this.

INDEPENDENT, INDEPENDENT CIRCUIT. Usually meaning not

plugged into a dimmer, but just switched on. A refrigerator light, for example, need not waste an important dimmer unless it is to dim. Just pick the correct wattage lamp.

INFRARED. Light with a wave length even shorter than red: too short a wave length to be seen.

INKY. *See* BABY SPOT—usually an inky is a tiny Fresnel.

INSTRUMENT. Usually a spot, striplight, etc.—but can be almost any device helping to produce or control the light.

INSTRUMENT SCHEDULE. A listing of the instruments in the light plot, describing their hardware, function, color, dimmer hookup, etc.

INSULATION. What wraps or surrounds or covers anything "live" so that you can touch it: non-conducting material such as rubber or asbestos.

INTENSITY. The voltage applied to the lamp. Usually, simply, the brightness of the light.

INTERLOCK. Mechanically connected dimmer handles that will work together when you move just one. Usually you can "lock" or "unlock" quickly.

IRIS. As in your camera lens, a device to open or close a hole to let more or less light through. In spotlight operator jargon, we say, "Iris in on her face".

JUICE. Electricity.

JUMPER. Short lengths of cable to connect—as opposed to long lengths of cable which also connect. Jumpers usually connect an instrument to a nearby receptacle.

JUNCTION BOX. *See* BOX.

KEY LIGHT. The light that will pick out the actor, or supply a sharp dramatic emphasis.

KEYSTONING. A projected image that distorts to a keystone shape because the surface is not at right angles to the lens. You see this with your slide projector. Often corrective lenses or a counter-distorted slide will correct this.

KILOWATT. 1,000 watts. A three-thousand-watt lamp or spotlight would usually be called a 3kw. A kilowatt hour is 1,000 watts used for one hour.

KLIEGLIGHT. Trade name: a big and powerful lighting instrument.

KNIFE SWITCH. Usually a pivoted arm that swings down and knifes into a metal holder, making contact. These can be large capacity and dangerously uninsulated.

LADDER. Looks like a metal ladder, standing or hung. The rungs are a fine place to clamp on instruments.

LAMP. The whole thing: filament or other source, glass globe (bulb), and base. Also can mean lighting instrument. As a verb, "Lamp those instruments!"

LAMP DIP. A heat-resistant and often light-resistant transparent lacquer for glass coloring which you can paint on to lamps—or dip them into. You might use it to paint projections.

LEADS. Usually the insulated wires coming out of an instrument, eager to be plugged in. "Pigtail" is used similarly. Also, vaguely, "cable lead".

LEKO, LEKOLIGHT. Trade name (Levy and Kook acronym) for a brand of Ellipsoidal Reflector Spot. Pronounced *Lee*-ko.

LENS. A glass or plastic piece that is curved in some way to shape (bend, condense) a beam of light.

LIGHT EFFICIENCY. How much of the electricity is turned into useful light.

LIGHT LEAK. Unwanted spill, unmasked backstage light, exit lights spoiling a blackout, etc.

LIGHT PLOT. A sheet or sheets showing your instruments and the information needed to hang and hook up and color them. Use and focus notes are not unwelcome.

LIMELIGHT. Old spotlight system whereby a flame heated up a chunk of limestone, which became hot and glowed brightly.

LINNEBACH PROJECTOR. A lamp in a big box, one side of which is a glass or plastic sheet on which you can execute a silhouette or simple painting and get a crude image projected. AKA shadow-graph projector.

LIVE. On. Hot. Carrying current.

LIVE FRONT. If the live parts are exposed and uninsulated, as in some boards and switch panels.

LOAD. The amount of electricity in a wire, dimmer, board, etc. It can be measured in Amperes or watts.

LOBSTERSCOPE. A device, usually a wheel, mounted in front of a lens. It has one or more slits in it, and when spun by hand or motor, creates a flicker.

LOUVRES, LOUVERS. Ventilating slots or baffles—air can circulate but light shouldn't leak. Or, Venetian blind-like louvers can be placed in front of the lens to cut spill, or to signal in Morse code.

LUMEN. An arbitrary measure of light, related to a foot candle. A measure of the delivered brightness from the light source.

MALE PLUG, MALE CONNECTOR. *See* FEMALE CONNECTORS.

MASTER CIRCUIT, MASTER DIMMER. A control for several other circuits, which feed through it.

MASTER SWITCH. The connection of a switchboard to the main power. A switch that cuts off all current to a board.

MAT. Another device to shape the beam, perhaps a cut-out stuck on front of the beam to cut spill or form a crude shadow projection.

MEMORY, MEMORY BOARD. A computer board that can store the cues and produce them again.

MOGUL (base). Bigger than the ordinary household lamp base—can be screw style, bipost, etc. Sometimes household three-way lamps have a mogul base.

MOTIVATION, MOTIVATED LIGHT. The apparently logical or explainable source for light on stage.

NEGATIVE. One of the directions in which current flows. The other is called positive.

NEON. A tube with a gas in it—electricity makes the gas glow.

OHM. An arbitrary measurement of electrical resistance, named after George Simon Ohm (1787–1854), a German physicist. For our purposes, the nature of the conducting wire: as few ohms as possible for the wire conducting electricity, plenty of ohms to impede it in a resistance dimmer.

OLIVETTE. Supposedly named after the musical show *Olivette*, this is a large box-like reflector, painted white, containing a big lamp. It's usually on a short floor stand in the wings, but can be hung, often just by chains, old-style.

OPERATOR. Spot Operator, Sound Operator, Board Operator. Or, sometimes, it may denote lesser status than "electrician", such as a person who plugs or unplugs something during a change.

OPTICAL SYSTEM. The components and relationship of the light source, reflector, lens.

OVERLOAD. Too much load for the wirings of the dimmer: perhaps too many lamps on a circuit. A fuse should blow before there's destruction such as melting or fire.

PAR (*Parabolic Aluminized Reflector*). The kind of lamp with its reflector moulded in. Identified by diameter: divide by 8. Thus a par 56 is seven inches in diameter.

PARABOLIC. One of the reflector shapes. Used mostly in beam projectors. The reflected rays are parallel.

PARALLEL, PARALLEL CIRCUIT. One way a circuit can be wired. First, the current flow is completed. Then the load (lamps, dimmers, etc.) can tap into it. In a SERIES CIRCUIT, the current must flow *through* each load unit to continue on its way. The eye of this storm appears each Christmas. Does the whole string blow when one lamp is stepped on?

PARCANS. A lighting instrument which is a housing for a PAR lamp. The housing has a yoke, color frame holders, etc.

PATCH PANEL. A panel where incoming leads (cables) from the instrument can be plugged into the dimmer of your choice.

PATCHING. Using the above device.

PHOSPHORESCENCE. Luminescence that continues *after* the charge by light, like a glowing watch dial. Biologically, it means light without an outside charge.

PIANO BOARD. One name for a resistance board, the kind we take on the road. It looks like an excited upright piano.

PIGTAIL. A connector on a short lead, usually the plug on short wires that comes out of the instrument.

PILOT LIGHT. Usually a light that shows that something is on.

PIN CONNECTOR. A common style of stage connector: at the end of a cable, a fiber block with holes or prongs. Sometimes you should tie the two cables in a simple overhand knot before making the connection, preventing this style of connector from pulling apart.

PIN SPOT. A narrow beam of light, also the instrument needed to produce it.

PIPE CLAMP. The clamp that attaches an instrument or arm to a pipe.

PIPE SIZES. The diameter is named by its inside opening: a one-inch pipe has a one-inch hole. It's about 1⅜" overall (outside) diameter, unless it's thin-walled. This nomenclature is an annoyance to us, who are concerned with the outside diameter, not the inside for water flow.

PIPE STAND. Vertical pipe and base for mounting instruments. Tie it off at top, if it's tall, for safety!

PLANO-CONVEX. A lens with one flat and one rounded surface.

PLASTICITY. Revealing the three-dimensional shape.

PLUG FUSE. The ordinary screw-in household fuse. Another familiar shape is cartridge, which is tubular and snaps in.

PLUGGING BOX. Old style receptacle, a hollow box, porcelainized, into which you push the male plug.

POLE. A positive or negative terminal.

PORTABLE BOARDS. Boards that can be carried with a touring show.

POSITIVE. *See* NEGATIVE.

PRACTICAL. A lighting unit onstage, from a flashlight to a table lamp, that really works. Usually means the lighting fixtures on a set, including jukeboxes, neon signs, chandeliers. If they don't light, they're set decorations: props.

PREFOCUS BASE. A notched lamp base that inserts and locks with a twist. It can be important to set the lamp precisely to place the filament in exact relationship to the reflector and lens.

PRE-SET. To set up a cue in advance. Also the dimmers or devices that do this.

PRIMARY COLORS. The light primaries are Blue, Green, and Red. In theory these can create all other colors.

PROJECTION. An image produced by a slide or film or cut-out.

PROJECTOR. Anything that can achieve the above, also refers to a BEAM PROJECTOR.

PROPORTIONAL DIMMING. If you interlock (physically connect) dimmers on an old resistance board and pull the handle down to half, for example, the dimmers that were full or more than half will be gathered mechanically and go down to half. Those already at half or less won't be affected. Your balance of light onstage could be upset. If you had done this electrically, by feeding all the dimmers through a huge one, the power reduction to all the dimmers would be 50 percent.

PUNCH. Brightness, pep, visibility. Usually combined with "plenty of" or "not enough"

QUARTZ. Bulbs that may have to resist great heat can be made of quartz instead of glass.

QUARTZ-HALOGEN. A lamp using some halogen gas. The gas, particularly iodine or bromine, reduces filament deterioration.

REACTANCE DIMMER. A dimmer using principles similar to those of the autotransformer dimmer.

READINGS. As in the phrase, "What's it reading?" meaning a dimmer, a light meter, etc. "What's the number setting?"

RECEPTACLE. What you plug into, but usually a fixed device, not the female plug on the end of another cable.

REFLECTOR. A surface that controls light by catching it and reflecting it.

REFRACTION. The bending of a light beam as it passes from one medium into another—air to glass, water, etc.

RELAY. A switch operated remotely by an electromagnet. Model train switches and accessories work this way.

RESISTANCE DIMMER. This dimmer works by adding resistance to the circuit. See Chapter 7.

RHEOSTAT. Similar to the above.

ROAD BOARD. Portable switchboard, usually meaning a piano board.

RONDEL, ROUNDEL. A moulded glass color filter, usually used in striplights.

SATURATION. Brightness of hue—degree of intensity of color. Not greyed down.

SCOOP. A lensless floodlight. It looks as if you'd dropped a lamp into an aluminium mixing bowl.

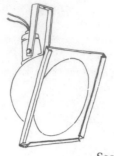

Scoop

SCREW BASE. Usual home-style screw-in lamp base. If the filament does not need exact placement, this can be used in theatre practice.

SEALED BEAM. A reflector lamp, similar to your auto headlights.

SERIES, SERIES CIRCUIT. *See* PARALLEL CIRCUIT.

SHARP FOCUS. A matter of importance in projections. In other practice, it is often poorly used. Instead of "spot focus". Some units can have a sharp or soft edge to their beam.

SHINBUSTER. A low-hung side light.

SHORT, SHORT CIRCUIT. The flow of electricity is fouled up by its conductor touching another conductor (your screwdriver or you, perhaps), or most commonly the negative and positive current touches without the proper resistance (a lamp) between them.

SHUTTERS. Gates that can close off light or shape the edge of the beam.

SIDEARM. A short pipe that clamps to a boom. The instrument hangs from the sidearm.

SNOOT. Another name for spill-preventers in front of a lens. *See* TOP HAT or FUNNEL.

SPECTRUM. Visible colored light falls within the spectrum, which carries up beyond red (infra-red) and below violet (ultraviolet). The wave lengths of this radiation are measured in angstroms, and the visible ones range from about 4,000 to about 7,000 angstroms.

SPHERICAL REFLECTOR. A reflector that is the shape of part of a globe. The filament (light source) is placed at its center.

SPILL. Light where you don't want it, caused by bad reflectors,

bad lenses, a hole in the side of the instrument. *Also see*
LIGHT LEAK.

SPLIT PLUG. Half-width stage plug so that two can go into one
receptacle, usually a plugging box. AKA HALF PLUG.

SPOTLIGHT, SPOT. Usually meaning an instrument with a lens.
ERS and Fresnels are the most commonly used.

SPREAD. The width that light from an instrument will
cover.

STAGE PLUG. Usually a plug at the end of a cable. It slides into
a dimmer receptacle. This is old road-board practice.

STAGE POCKET. Receptacle for a plug or plugs.

STAND. Usually a floor stand holding a spotlight, a loudspeaker,
a microphone. Can be portable. A boom implies taller and
not portable.

STEP LENS. Similar to a Fresnel lens. Often used in ERS.

STRIP (as a verb). This is spotlight talk—"strip" means to change
from a round beam to wide-stage coverage. Opening the
iris and letting the shutters take over can allow these rectangular beam shapes.

STRIPLIGHT, STRIP. A troughlike housing containing many
lamps in a row.

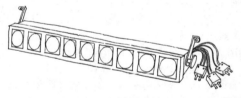

Striplight

SUB MASTER. A dimmer through which other dimmers feed,
and it controls them—but it's not the biggest—*see* GRAND
MASTER.

SURPRISE PINK. A frequently used color of gel or plastic—it's a
lavender that seems warm if contrasted with cool gels, and
cool if opposed to warms.

SWITCH. Device or action to break or complete a circuit.

SWITCHBOARD. Dimmer board, control board. Where you dim
the lights and so forth. See Chapter 7.

TEMPLATE. A pattern usually cut out of metal that will project its silhouette if put in some spotlights, usually ellipsoidals.

TERMINAL. A place in an electric line where a switch or a connector is placed.

TEST LAMP. Usually a low-wattage lamp we touch to a circuit to find out if current is passing through. We can track down where the circuit is broken.

THROW. How far an instrument (light beam) will effectively reach. You can also throw a switch.

THYRATRON. A part of one of the electronic dimmers. A sort of trigger or gate (very fast) in a gas-filled tube.

TINT. Not saturated—a paled color.

TONING. A wash of color lighting as opposed to spotlighting.

TORMENTOR (TORMS). Usually meaning scenery, but can mean the lights downstage, usually a vertical row of lights downstage on either side of the proscenium.

TOP HAT. *See* FUNNEL. This style looks like a blown-out top hat—the rim is what slides into the color-frame holder.

TOP LIGHT. Light from above the actor. Usually implying that the purpose is to give a body an edge, a halo. This helps to pick it out of the background.

TOWER. Vertical mounting position for lights. Can be substantial, such as permanent torms.

TRANSMISSION. Usually means how much light passes through a partial barrier such as a color filter.

TREE. A light stand or boom with horizontal "branches" for attaching (hanging) instruments.

TRIP. A circuit breaker trips when the circuit overheats, and can be re-set when it cools.

TWIST-LOCK. Connecting plugs where the parts twist during joining so that they are locked together. "Twistlock" is a trademarked name that is often misused in this general way.

TWOFER. Two female plugs joined to one male—thus two cables can be joined into one circuit.

ULTRAVIOLET. Light below the visible violet—its wave length is too long to see. We use it to make certain colors and coatings glow in the dark—they are excited by the light waves invisible to us. *See* FLORESCENCE.

UNIT. Lighting instrument.

VOLT. Arbitrary unit of electrical force, named after Count Alessandro Volta (1745–1827), Italian.

VOLTAGE DROP. Current that arrives weak because of a too-long journey, or too-small wires or cables, or bad connections.

WALL POCKET. *See* STAGE POCKET. Need not be recessed, but sometimes is. WALL SOCKET is about the same, but usually implies household use instead of stage current.

WARM. Colors such as red, yellow, amber, orange.

WATT. Arbitrary unit of electrical power, named after James Watt (1736–1819), Scottish. These units all sound the same, but they are different. If it helps, know that a Watt is the work done by a current of one Ampere under the pressure of one Volt.

WIRE. Noun—the conducting metal strand. Also a verb, as in "wiring a circuit".

WORKLIGHT. This helps you see during set-ups and rehearsals. You may have to be able to switch it on in a quick change. "Under Worklight" is the phrase for rehearsal without stage crew. The cry "Works!" is what ends the show for me: the curtain is down after the last bow.

XENON LAMP. A lamp with an arc arrangement in it. Xenon gas is in there to help. You don't have to "feed" it.

X-RAY. Originally a trademark name for a reflector which was used in show window lighting. Later it was used in striplights. Sometimes used to mean the big trough of uncolored, uncompartmented lamps, comprising a worklight or concert border, but good striplights are often called X-rays.

YOKE. The U-shaped holder embracing a lighting unit like sugar tongs around a lump.

Index to Quotations

Agee, James. *Let Us Now Praise Famous Men*. With Walker Evans. Boston: Houghton Mifflin and Co., 1941.

Akutagawa, Ryunoseuke. *Rashomon and Other Stories*. Translated by Takashi Kojima. New York: Liveright, 1970.

Belloc, Hilaire. *The Cruise of the Nona*. New York: Penguin Books, 1958.

Bellow, Saul. *Humboldt's Gift*. New York: Viking, 1975.

Blake, William. "The Marriage of Heaven and Hell", in *The Portable Blake*. New York: Viking, 1946.

Bowen, Elizabeth. *The Death of the Heart*. New York: Knopf, 1939.

Brontë, Charlotte. *Jane Eyre*. New York: Collier Books, 1962.

Byron (George Gordon, Lord Byron). *A Self-Portrait: Letters and Diaries, 1798 to 1824*, vol. 2. Edited by Peter Quennell. London: John Murray, 1950.

Camus, Albert. *The Plague*. Translated by Stuart Gilbert. New York: Vintage, 1972.

Capote, Truman. "Tangier", in *The Dogs Bark*. New York: Random House, 1973.

le Carré, John. *The Spy Who Came in from the Cold*. New York: Coward-McCann, 1963.

Cary, Joyce. *The Horse's Mouth*. New York: Harper and Brothers, 1944.

Cheever, John. *Falconer*. New York: Knopf, 1977.

Childers, Erskine. *The Riddle of the Sands*. London: Rupert Hart-Davis, 1969.

Conrad, Joseph. *The Mirror of the Sea*. New York: Doubleday, 1926.

Dennison, George. *The Lives of Children*. New York: Random House, 1969.

Dickens, Charles. *Great Expectations*. New York: Bantam, 1981.

Dinesen, Isak. "The Monkey", in *Seven Gothic Tales*. New York: The Modern Library, 1934.

Dostoyevsky, Fyodor. *Crime and Punishment*. Translated by David Magarshack. Baltimore: Penguin Books, 1973.

Doyle, Sir Arthur Conan. "The Hound of the Baskervilles", in *The Complete Sherlock Holmes*. New York: Garden City Publishing Co., 1938.

Durrell, Lawrence. *Mountolive*. New York: E.P. Dutton & Co., Inc., 1959.

Faulkner, William. "The Bear", in *Three Famous Short Novels*. New York: Random House, 1942.

Flaubert, Gustave. *Madame Bovary.* Translated by Alan Russell. New York: Penguin Books, 1977.

Gibson, Walter. *The Weird Adventures of the Shadow.* New York: Grosset and Dunlap, 1966.

Greenberg, Joanne. *High Crimes and Misdemeanors.* New York: Holt, Rinehart and Winston, 1977.

Greene, Graham. *Travels with My Aunt.* New York: Viking, 1969.

Herbert, Frank. *Dune.* New York: Berkley Medallion, 1977.

Hersey, John. *Hiroshima.* New York: Knopf, 1946.

Hesse, Herman. *Steppenwolf.* Translated by Basil Creighton. New York: Holt, Rinehart and Winston, 1963.

Jewett, Sarah Orne. *The Country of the Pointed Firs.* New York: Doubleday, 1956.

Kawabata, Yasunari. *Snow Country.* Translated by Edward G. Seidensticker. New York: Knopf, 1969.

Keller, Helen, *The Story of My Life.* New York: Doubleday, 1954.

Kerouac, Jack. *The Town and the City.* London: Quartet, 1950.

Kingston, Maxine Hong. *The Woman Warrior: Memoirs of a Girlhood among Ghosts.* New York: Vintage, 1975.

Kipling, Rudyard. *Captains Courageous.* New York: Bantam Books, 1966.

Lewis, Richard. "Journeys", in *Prose by Children of the English Speaking World.* Collected by Richard Lewis. New York: Simon and Schuster, 1969.

Mann, Thomas. "Tristan", in *Stories of Three Decades.* Translated by H. T. Lowe-Porter. New York: Knopf, 1936.

Marquez, Gabriel Garcia. *The Autumn of the Patriarch.* New York: Avon, 1977.

McCullers, Carson. "The Member of the Wedding", in *The Ballad of the Sad Café.* Cambridge, Mass.: The Riverside Press, 1951.

Melville, Herman. *Moby Dick, or The White Whale.* New York: Dodd, Mead & Co., 1942.

Mishima, Yukio. *The Sound of Waves.* Translated by Meredith Weatherby. New York: Berkley Medallion, 1971.

Nabokov, Vladimir. *The Gift.* Translated by Michael Scammell with collaboration of the author. New York: Putnam's Sons, 1963.

Nathan, Robert. *One More Spring.* New York: Knopf, 1933.

Pasternak, Boris. *Doctor Zhivago.* Translated by Max Hayward and Manya Harari. New York: Pantheon, 1958.

Proust, Marcel. *Swann's Way.* Translated by C. K. Scott Moncrieff. New York: The Modern Library, 1928.

Renault, Mary. *The Last of the Wine.* New York: Random House, 1975.

Schulberg, Budd. *What Makes Sammy Run?* New York: Random House, 1941.

Singer, Isaac Bashevis. *In My Father's Court.* New York: Fawcett Crest, 1966.

Slocum, Captain Joshua. *Sailing Alone around the World*. New York: Dover Publications, 1956.

Steinbeck, John. *The Grapes of Wrath*. New York: Bantam Books, 1972.

Stuckey, P. J. *The Sailing Pilots of the Bristol Channel*. London: David and Charles, 1977.

Tanizaki, Junichiro. *The Makioka Sisters*. Translated by Edward G. Seidensticker. Tokyo: Tuttle, 1970.

Thomas, Dylan. *Quite Early One Morning*. New York: New Directions, 1960.

Thomas, Lewis. "An Apology", from *The Medusa and the Snail*, New York: Bantam Books.

Thoreau, Henry David. "The Headwaters of the Allegash", in *The Maine Woods*. New York: Bramhau House, undated.

Thurber, James. "The Topaz Cufflinks Mystery", in *The Thurber Carnival*. New York: The Modern Library, 1945.

Timothy. See Lewis, Richard.

Twain, Mark. *Life on the Mississippi*. New York: Harper and Brothers, 1923.

Virgil. *The Aeneid*. Translated by W. F. Jackson Knight. New York: Penguin Books, 1956.

Welty, Eudora. *Losing Battles*. New York: Vintage, 1978.

White, E. B. "The Ring of Time," in *Essays of E. B. White*. New York: Harper and Row, 1977.

White, T. H. *The Once and Future King*, New York: Berkeley Publishing Corp., 1981.

Wolfe, Thomas. *Of Time and the River*. New York: Scribner's Sons, 1935.

Yourcenar, Marguerite. *Memoirs of Hadrian*. New York: Farrar, Strauss and Company, 1963.